Reframing
Spiritual Formation

Reframing
Spiritual Formation
Discipleship in an Unchurched Culture

Edward H. Hammett

SMYTH&HELWYS
PUBLISHING, INCORPORATED • MACON, GEORGIA

Smyth & Helwys Publishing, Inc.
6316 Peake Road
Macon, Georgia 31210-3960
1-800-747-3016
©2002 by Smyth & Helwys Publishing
All rights reserved.
Printed in the United States of America.

Edward H. Hammett

The paper used in this publication meets the minimum
requirements of American National Standard for Information
Sciences—Permanence of Paper for Printed Library
Materials. ANSI Z39.48–1984. (alk. paper)

Library of Congress Cataloging-in-Publication Data

Hammett, Edward H.
        Reframing Spiritual Formation: Discipleship in an
        Unchurched Culture / Edward H. Hammett
        p.   cm.
        Includes bibliographical references.
        1. Church education.
        2. Secularism.
        3. Church Renewal.
        I. Title.
        BV1467.H28   2002
        2628—dc21

                                                        2001055129
                                                        CIP

ISBN 1-57312-375-7 (pbk.)

Inclusion of various websites does not indicate personal endorsement.

Contents

Acknowledgments

Becoming an author is a surprise to me and to many of my friends. The creation and development of all three of my books have been tied to my life experiences and the growth edges in my spiritual pilgrimage.

I am very grateful to those persons mentioned in the manuscript who have in so many ways been used of God to teach me how to relate to and nurture those spiritually thirsty persons who do not or can not find their place in church. There are so many who are asking life's spiritual questions but are not attracted by or assimilated into our churches. Their spiritual formation is important too. I am grateful for how their thirst for meaning, hope and healing have touched my life. I am grateful for how their spiritual journey helped inform my journey as a "professional clergy" who is seeking to assist churches understand and penetrate our increasingly secular and unchurched world.

I continue to be touched and blessed by Findley and Louvenia Edge, Bill and Bettie Clemmons, Len Sweet, Bill Easum, Tom Bandy and Mary and Gordon Cosby. Their ministries in print and their tender touches of friendship and accountability will always be of value to me in my spiritual formation and is something I am learning not to take for granted.

I am also very grateful for the Baptist State Convention of North Carolina who continues to encourage my writing and my walking of the cutting edges in denominational life and Christian education. Many of my colleagues nurture my dreams and ideas while others offer deep and passionate challenges of my dreams and ideas. Both perspectives have meaning in my journey.

For those who have read and re-read this manuscript in its preparation I am grateful. David, Connie, Bill, Chuck, Randy, and Suzanne have been helpful in clarifying ideas, finding the appropriate language and keeping me focused and honest.

For those who lend their endorsement to this work I am deeply grateful for I know they are lending their credibility and encouragement. I do not take this lightly and find great hope and nurture in their willingness to share their name and their time to this project.

Last, but certainly not least, I am grateful for Smyth & Helwys for again taking a risk on my writings. They continue to offer assistance, encouragement, and an opportunity to share my ideas. Thanks also goes to Keith Gammons, my new editor. My manuscript was waiting on him as he arrived at his new job. Thanks Keith for your skilled assistance.

—Edward H. Hammett

Foreword
A Disciple's Life of Learning

*In times of change the learner shall inherit the earth, while the
learned will be equipped for a world that no longer exists.*
         —novelist James Thurber

People can be divided into two groups: the learned and the learners.
The learned I call "skulls": at a certain point early in life, the skull
gets as big as it's going to get. The skull freezes in the form it's in for
the rest of its life.

The learners I call "ears": up until the day you die, your ears
keep growing. (Check out singer Tony Bennett's ears sometime.) The
difference between "skulls" people and "ears" people is that skulls
have minds that have closed and fused shut, while ears keep asking
new questions and are not afraid to face new challenges. Ears try to
learn from the past rather than instruct the past on where it has
gone wrong.

The 21st century needs ears. Nine months after the century was
birthed, its first child was born: 11 September 2001. Nine-Eleven
has been called a massive "failure of intelligence," or as Newsweek
corrected it, a failure of imagination (did anyone even imagine its
possibility?). The failure of our "intelligence" agencies created a security crisis that resulted in the deaths of thousands of people from
over 60 countries.

But the failure of our "intelligence" agencies like the CIA (whose
skullish name reveals part of the problem: only decentralized intelligence can win "netwars") tells only a small story in a much larger
drama. There is a whole new world out there. And if we are not all
to become literal skulls, the learned must become learners.

The first step in becoming an ear is to admit that what used to
work no longer does. Air Force General Richard Myers, nominated
in August 2001 to be chairman of the Joint Chiefs of Staff, admits
to being trained and educated "for a different war than we're in."
President George W. Bush confesses our need to "come to terms
with the new realities of our world."

What should be our responses to these "intelligence failures?" We can rail against leaders who have let us down by not coming to terms with these new realities. We can lament our decades-long vulnerability to attack caused by leaders who have spent hundreds of billions of dollars a year preparing us for everything but the real world and the real dangers we face.

Or we can grow some ears. The government's colossal failure to insure our safety as citizens is only matched by the church's failure to gird and guard its members in patterns of discipleship that can faithfully follow Christ into this new world. In fact, the very Nine-Eleven crisis was more an expression of one man's attempt to convert other Muslims to his brand of Islamic faith than an attempt to bring the western world down. The struggle going on in the Muslim world right now is how to define one's faith for a new world.

This crisis of spiritual intelligence is also a struggle in the Christian world. We can lack intelligence in more ways than one. How many religious leaders admit to being trained to do ministry for a world that no longer exists? Christian churches are filled pastors whose role has taught them to be "teachers" and laity whose role in the church and business world has taught them to be "students." The problem of religious leadership is that while laity are more prone to be ears than skulls, clergy are more prone to be skulls than ears. Hence the current problem of ecclesiastical gridlock. Have you ever experienced "gridlock" on the highway. There is such a thing as mental and spiritual gridlock that can be even more difficult to get out of than physical gridlock.

Eddie Hammett wants us to be an ears-Christian not a skull-Christian. In the spirit of Paul, who towards the end of his life admitted that he still did not comprehend it all ("I do not reckon myself to have got hold of it yet" Phil 13:13–NEB), Hammett has presented this book to us as an exercise in intelligence gathering. It gets us out of our gridlocked state by showing us how the life of Christ is a life of learning. In this sense it is a very Hebrew book. For the ancient Hebrews learning and scholarship were themselves religious activities.

This is also a book that also teaches us how to face the biggest challenges facing the world today. What are these realities confronting the globe? They're not the glitzy new problems that attend the advent of a new world, as real and big as they are. Rather, they're the grizzly problems of human nature that are as old as Adam and Eve.

—Leonard Sweet
Drew Theological School
George Fox Evangelical Seminary
preachingplus.com

Preface—A Rude Personal Awakening and My Personal and Professional Faith Challenge

Introduction

Life is full of twists, challenges, shocks, griefs, celebrations, and joys woven within an array of relationships. The arrival of the 21st century has dumped additional pressures upon an already challenging life. Now we have a multitude of advances made in technology, communications, bio-ethics, and medicine, as well as ecological concerns and terrorist threats that are calling for a hosts of dysfunctional persons to make clear decisions that will impact future generations. In the midst of all of this, and so much more, the church's Christian education ministry has remained mostly unchanged and unchallenged. Most churches continue to believe and practice Christian education that is done in classrooms, driven by printed literature, and tied to institutional loyalty and preservation. Attendance in many church programs has been on the decline in most major denominations for over a decade. We have surmised that this drop in participation and excitement was due to secularization of our materialistic culture or the apathy of our church members. Could it be that the primary problem is not with the people, but with the programs and with the churches?

Personal Experiences Calling for Reframing of Christian Education

The following situations are personal encounters I have had over the years, inside and outside local churches, that suggest that a *reframing* is desperately needed if Christians are to grow in faith, life skills, and relationships as we move through various life stages/experiences in our high-tech world:

• Parents, siblings, and friends are stunned by the divorces of their children, siblings or friends. Such shock leaves them hurting, confused, and drained. Evidently the church doesn't want to get involved. Few, if any, call or invite them into a redemptive, caring conversation. They and the divorcing feel alienated/isolated at the time they need people the most. The church has little to offer in divorce recovery, grief management, relationship management, and reconciliation. There are not even any current or appropriate educational resources in the church media center. It's almost as if the church isn't interested in these stresses of life and the faith isn't related to tough times.

• A young Christian lady explains that she and her husband decided to abort a pregnancy because of health threat to the mother and possibly the child. Grief, confusion, anger, and agony welled up as they sought to find redemption, forgiveness for themselves, from God and from each other. They needed a funeral to acknowledge the birth and validate the emotions and the child — but the church wasn't there. For months they were even afraid to share the information for fear of condemnation and judgment. They felt bad enough and just couldn't take the risk.

• A young Christian man has been living with the tug of homosexual behavior and thoughts in his lifestyle for almost a decade. The tugs have become more and more intense, the life complications become more testy and the church isn't there. He is afraid to even bring it up for fear of judgment, condemnation, and misunderstanding so he lives with it and eventually complicates his world even further when he is diagnosed with HIV. It is clear to him and to his family, from the frequent jokes and judgments made in church by church people in their presence, that the church can not or will not be of any help to them.

• A grandmother and mother heard of their relative's HIV status and their faith was thrown into a tailspin. A roller coaster of emotions, fears, concerns, anger at God, the relative, the doctors, the others involved, and the church and there was no avenue for working with, confessing, or understanding within the context of the faith these life experiences.

- A mother dies a painful death after being bedridden for years and the only daughter discovers her anger at God and the church because it appears that both were on vacation after about the first two months of her mom's illness. No one calls, no one offers respite care for the exhausted caregivers. The cards come, but no one wants to invest in the "messiness of our lives." She can't even do the funeral in the church, because she is so angry — and there is no place of redemption — only defensiveness in and by the church.

- A young man makes his first million dollars by 30 years old and experiences uncommon feelings, pressures, and challenges. He wants help in being a good steward of the resources and only finds a "greedy church that wants to build bigger buildings rather than help needy people." Such disappointment fuels his growing skepticism rather than walking with him through a new rite of passage.

- A Christian young adult and faithful church leader who is in a faith crisis finds the church wanting much from him — his leadership, his gifts, his time, his energy, his money — and without preparation or willingness to help him through his painful and persistent faith crisis.

- A young woman desiring to break unhealthy cycles in life caused by an alcoholic father and a mother who died when the young woman was a preschooler couldn't find a church to "work with faith and life issues." All she found at church was judgment, harsh ridicule, and advice to "pray about it and keep going." She needed and wanted someone to validate her faith journey and point her to scriptures and principles to help her find healing, hope and meaning once again. Instead she found irrelevant sermons, literature, classes, and programs. They were answering questions this young woman wasn't asking.

- A newlywed couple buys their first home and wants to dedicate it to God. The church offers no help.

- A new business owner wants to dedicate his business, and employees to God. The church offers no help.

- A family moves into their new home, which was rebuilt after a major fire. They want to recommit themselves and their new home to God. The church is of little help.

- A young couple wants to thank God, the physicians, and medical community for bringing their premature baby through a difficult time. The church is of little help.

- A young person is pregnant out of wedlock and desires to commit her life and child to God and the church will not let them participate in parent/child dedication services.

- A single parent desires to dedicate their "test tube child" and the church dismisses the request because there is no father and they disapprove of the way the child was conceived.

- A faithful Christian family discovers their unwed young adult daughter is pregnant. Their personal grief, shock, embarrassment, and guilt not only chew at their health and emotional stability, but is eroding their faith system. They just can't tell their Christian friends. They just can't tell their pastors and church leaders. Such deep embarrassment prevents them from reaching out and the church, even though they know something is happening due to their absences from church, don't know how to reach in. Such a stalemate creates hostility and anger in their household. When the daughter begins to show they can't hide it anymore and they leave the church.

How might Christian education be reframed to be more relevant in the messy times of life, in those times when life has lost its meaning or purpose, when pain is more paramount each day than pleasure, when a joy is so great that a blessing needs to mark it? How can Christian education assist us with the "landmarks and land mines" of life?

Christian education needs to:

• be built on life experiences/stages.
• create experiences that mark the rites of passage in the pleasures and pains of life.
• create experiences which network believers and others on a spiritual journey, around common life experiences.
• create forums for theological reflection for persons involved in similar life experiences.
• create worship/validation experiences designed to help persons confess, rebuild, and mark life's significant pleasures and pains.
• create accountability, support relationships, and curricula to help persons take the next step in the faith and life journey.

It is my purpose here to expound on these and other concepts — to offer some new structures and principles for reframing *discipleship* in a secular culture. This is not a broad-based research driven project, and it's certainly not intended to be comprehensive. Rather I'm sharing avenues that God has allowed me to travel to learn from and grow through. The avenues I'll chart include "Why Reframe Discipleship?", "Challenges to Reframing," and "Discipleship That Matters in an Unchurched Culture." I offer these as thoughts to ponder, pray over and consider as we all seek to be all that God desires us to be in this rapidly changing world.

—Edward Hammett
Hendersonville, NC
August 12, 2001

Why Reframe Discipleship?

Church in the New Century?

As the new millennium begins I find myself asking if the institutional church I know and love will be a relevant and driving force in the new century. The question has intense personal implications for me. As 1999 came to an end and much of the world anticipated the joys of Christmas celebration, the joys of Hanukkah or the traditions of Kwanza, I encountered a different set of emotions. I awoke in the predawn hours on Christmas Eve morning, turned on the television, and discovered that a young couple had been murdered. I knew the community and because of the commentator's description, I feared I might also know the couple. You see, the couple's marriage was shaky because of the husband's gambling addiction. He had gambled them into indescribable debt before he ever shared it with his wife. I was so troubled that I went ahead and got up, prayed, did my morning devotion, and prepared to go shopping with my brother for his son's Christmas gift.

As we drove to Toys R Us, he took us the long way so that he could share with me that he and his wife would be separating after Christmas. What a shock! From all indications they had the perfect marriage. New house, new cars, new furniture, new baby, excellent jobs, good friends, good church, supportive families, yet I heard him say they had grown apart. Following this tearful conversation, we bought the gift and returned home. He asked me to hold his confidence until they shared with the other family members after Christmas. We went to church, celebrated Christmas, silent communion and worship, but in deep pain searching for a handle which was not found.

I returned home from Sunday worship and heard of a friend's young unmarried daughter who was pregnant out of wedlock. She had decided to have an abortion and shared this with her parents prior to Christmas. They are all very committed churchgoers, active in church leadership for years and they too found nothing for their Christmas trauma.

I then talked with another friend who was struggling with the realities of facing Christmas in his dysfunctional family. Tense emotions surrounded becoming "mom's little boy again even though he's 42 years old." And then there is the unchurched friend, seeking Christ and community, struggling to untangle relationships, break unhealthy patterns, and learn new life-skills to help insure a healthier life in the twenty-first century.

None of us seemed to be able to find help, hope, or support for our life crises at church. Certainly, we found a place of worship and that is important, but we needed guidance, specific support, and community to face and grow through life's heartaches and struggles. I found myself wondering about church and the twenty-first century. As life becomes more complex and challenging, can the church create effective ministry?

What did we need from the church at these crises points? Our consensus was:

- A trustworthy, safe community of believers
- Mentoring relationships of those who had gone before and were willing to "walk with" those hurting and seeking God in the midst of crises
- A support group to help us with nurture, understanding and accountability as we seek health and wholeness
- Persons who would commit to consistent support and encouragement.
- Opportunities to reflect on new life lessons in light of biblical truths
- Opportunities to deal with life issues and lessons in the context of worship (confession, intercession, healing, forgiveness, praise, gratitude, etc.)
- Forums designed to help us turn our pains into ministry avenues

Assessing the Past and Planning for the Future

Christian education in the church of the twenty-first century will not be dictated as much by Arthur Flake's organizational formulas or age grading a Sunday School as it will by helping believers and non-believers identify life's lessons, rites of passage, and integration of information into soul making. *What will grow a church numerically will be how well a church masters the art of integration of spiritual lessons around real life needs.* Hurting and wandering people are seeking direction and will show up and be committed to relationships and opportunities that move them forward from pain to purpose, from struggle to success, from hopelessness to hope, from confusion to conviction, and from loneliness to loving relationships. Walking the journey with people through life's challenges becomes the essence of curriculum. Discovering the pressing questions around new life lessons and fashioning a road to biblically based answers to these questions becomes the primary rubric of organization.

The difficulty many will have with this is that this model of Christian education is not as institutionally dependent as our former models of Christian education. (By the way, a look at church history will reveal that its really only in the last 300 years that we have become so institutionally dependent.) I do not believe it negates the need for institutions, but it certainly changes their dominant place in our organizational structure for Christian education. If we take this model seriously, many of our churches, as presently designed, will likely only be used to their maximum potential once a month or even less frequently. (That is, unless we begin to partner with other community based nonprofit organizations.) The relational educational groupings will likely best be done in casual, informal settings and then a time of worship, praise, and accountability will be at one time in a corporate event.

Now let me be quick to say I think there is much to learn about how to design church buildings or faith community centers for effectiveness in the future. Our sanctuary may become a small room with a circle of chairs and relevant symbols of our faith that is visited at need by persons seeking similar answers or support. Our worship center may become a rented or shared community building auditorium. Educational and mission sites may become our worksites, schools, community clubs, recreational settings, etc. as believers become more intentional in their daily walks and learning to teach, preach, and baptize "as we go." Seems like that is a mandate our Lord left with us.

Such a transition certainly calls forth a different set of skills, expectations, and requirements of "church members." The implications are many for our policies and practices of church membership, leadership election and training, budgeting and the role of clergy and our facilities. Another area this shift challenges is the way we define success or effectiveness. (See my *The Gathered and Scattered Church* for many ideas to help reframe these standards.)

Somehow we must remember that in the history of religious education, printed curriculum for the masses did not emerge until after the printing press invention. Before that it was built on life issues, life lessons, and the community experiences as they sought God in their midst. The family was critically important and responsible as instructors of the faith. The old were to teach the young and the faith formation gatherings were more informal than institutionally driven. The early New Testament church found its nurture and education in house churches at times the members could gather.

Since we are back in a very similar cultural environment as that of the book of Acts, maybe it's time to rethink and reframe. Since our print media is now challenged by multimedia, maybe it's time to

Reframing Hints To Ponder

- What people need from the institutional church must be relevant to life issues and passages
- Christian education in the church of the twenty-first century will not be dictated as much by Arthur Flake's organizational formulas or age grading a Sunday School as it will by helping believers and non-believers identify life's lessons, rites of passage and integration of information into soulmaking
- Walking the journey with people through life's challenges becomes the essence of curriculum
- Discovering the pressing questions around new life lessons and fashioning a road to biblically based answers to these questions becomes the primary rubric of organization

rethink and reframe. Since our life needs and situations are confronted with greater complexity in an ever-changing culture, maybe it's time to rethink and reframe.

When the Church Pursues Sinners (Reflections on Luke 15)

"If the church is going to accomplish her divinely inspired purpose in a postmodern world, it must do some restructuring," is a basic conclusion of Randy Frazee, pastor of Pantego Bible Church and author of *The Connecting Church*.[1] George Barna, a Christian researcher, clarifies this when he says his research indicates the church is a high control institution and the unchurched are persons who demand control. They don't want people telling them what to do. Such immediately puts the churched and the unchurched in conflict. The unchurched also say they are not especially spiritual, rather more theologically liberal, and they are not terribly interested in the church — however, they are aware of their personal deficiencies.[2]

The church is in serious trouble. Attendance is on the decline in most major denominations; commitment of the core leaders is waning; the leadership core is aging rapidly; and most churches are not reaching the new and younger generation. Consequently many are suggesting that in 20 years or less many churches will "go out of business" because there will be neither tithers nor leaders for existing programs. The harried lives of Americans are leading persons to become more selective in what they give their time and energies too. To many church is no longer a high priority — the church is seen as irrelevant or something that can be supplanted by other arenas or relationships.

While this is the prevalent atmosphere of our day, the biblical command of Matthew 28:19-20 to reach the world still stands. God's mission will be accomplished — even if God has to choose another people again. It seems that many churches have created or at least contributed to the apathy and malaise of our day by focusing more on pampering those in the pews rather than reaching those in the world. Many current church leaders believe that the clergy are there to "take care of them," when in reality the biblical role of the clergy is to "equip the saints for the work of ministry" (Eph 4). The introversion of many churches must change if the church is to thrive again and bring pleasure to our God's heart. The church must learn to pursue sinners as Jesus did.

Barriers to Pursuing Sinners

Because church people have become so comfortable with being cared for and being the center of attention when decisions are to be made, it will be difficult to shift to pursuing sinners as a primary function/mission of the church. Luke 15 and the parable of the Prodigal provide an excellent biblical framework for these thoughts.

Note first the parable was about and to the religious people — the Pharisees (15:1-2). Because Jesus was not paying enough attention to them, they began to "mutter" (v. 2). At this muttering Jesus "told them" — the religious people — the parables (v. 3). He reminds them that the shepherd leaves the flock to find the one lost sheep. *What?* Leaving the church people to pursue the lost? How many pastors and church leaders hold this value system and act upon it?

Many churches and church people are judgmental toward the sinner — as if those inside the church fold were pure as the driven snow. As in the parable of the Prodigal, grace does not come naturally to the human family — whether we are inside or outside the fold. The prodigal son's brother was not forgiving at all — in fact he was very judgmental of his father and his brother — even after his younger brother "came to his senses" and desired to come home (15:25-29). How much like this has the church been toward the sinners in our community — those who have strayed, missed the mark, disobeyed, however we choose to describe those outside the church and outside the faith?

Yes, if we are going to reach those outside the church, the church will not only have to restructure our programming and organization, we will have to repent of our judgmental spirits and our selfishness and self-centeredness. Ouch! These words do hurt, but in many of our hearts and churches they are true. Our repentance as the people of God is essential if the church is to rebuild respect and relationships among those outside the faith and the church.

Learning to Pursue Sinners

The church has spent decades learning to pamper our pews, resource our saints, and build our programs and facilities to meet our needs and desires. Now the realities of our secular age, the clarity of the biblical commands, and the survival of the church we love depends on the church learning what it means to pursue sinners rather than sustain saints. Again, let me be clear. I am not suggesting that we manipulate the unchurched into our churches so they will survive. I am suggesting that we learn to practice compassion, patience, tolerance, grace, mercy, and unconditional love to those who are hurting, aimless, lonely, lost, searching, hopeless, helpless, and reaching out. While this is frightening to many and hints at "compromising the Gospel" to others, it seems to me it is akin to the earthly ministry of Jesus. Yes, it's risky. Yes, it's radical. Yes, it's different than the norm most of us grew up with. Yes, it will revolutionize the way we do church. Yes, I believe it is the call of Christ for the people of God to minister in this secular age.

What does it mean to the people of God if we are serious about learning to pursue sinners — not for our gain, but for their wholeness, health and healing? Let me make a few suggestions:

- Churches need to pay careful attention to the language we use and the attitudes we project in our promotion, worship services, outreach efforts, socials, and curricula. (Maybe we need a proof reader from the unchurched world to help sensitize us to barriers we are erecting between the faith and the nonbeliever by the language we use or the promotion we do without thinking carefully of how the unchurched or unbeliever will hear or view this.)

- Churches are challenged to create comfortable, nonthreatening entry points for the sinners rather than for those of us inside the church family. This requires a change of mindset of leaders, refocusing of some of our budget and personnel energies. (Maybe every workteam in your church needs someone who is an advocate or voice for the non-believer or unchurched person to help keep us balanced in our ministries.)

- Rethinking our facilities, our programming, our schedules, and our openness to diversity of values, traditions, rituals and family structures. Again, let me be clear. I'm not pleading for embracing nonChristian lifestyles or values — I am pleading that we practice the Christian virtues of our Lord as he approached the woman at the well (John 4).

- Maybe we need to free some of the believers and church leaders time from "church activities and positions" and encourage them and affirm them for building redemptive, healthy relationships with non-believers and the unchurched. This is a real shift of values for many and a new standard of success for churches. It's not how many church meetings you come to or how many church positions you hold that make you faithful and honorable as a believers. Rather it is how many nonbelievers you build redemptive relationships with and how many you nurture into the faith. (For additional information about this issue see my *The Gathered and Scattered Church*.) Far too many church leaders do not even know the names of non-believers. In a secular world this must change if the faith is to be experienced and embraced by those outside our churches.

Lessons for the Church from the Prodigal Son

I've faced some hard realities about the church, myself and the arrogance, self-righteousness and self-centeredness that many of us tend to fall into before we even know it. Such narcissistic behavior has, over the last decades of the churches ministry, built barriers rather than bridges to those Christ loves and calls us as His people to reach. The parable of the prodigal son calls us, as the people of God — the religious leaders — to face some tough lessons that will certainly stretch many of us far beyond our comfort zone. Notice with me the lessons learned in the story of the prodigal that will help the church and the believer move forward in effectiveness and faith in our secular age:

- Be patient with lost people. Christians, like the prodigal's older brother, seem to be long on anger and short on mercy. Even though we may be offended by a lifestyle or behavior of a sinner, we are challenged to be patient not judgmental.
- Don't give up on sinners to easy or too early. The prodigal's father watched from afar and waited patiently praying that his son would come to his senses.

• Find a way to restore the fallen — the lost. The prodigal's father ran after his dirty, smelly son and restored him.

What venues, ministries and entry points do we have that helps us as the people of God be faithful to these lessons that help pursue the sinners, redeem the lost, and restore those who've strayed away and been caught by the "wilds" of the secular age?

It is my hope and prayer that this manuscript might help us discuss, learn about and embrace some new learning that will deepen our faith walk with Christ, improve the effectiveness of our churches and personal ministries and that the saints and the sinners might find viable fulfilling pathways of spiritual formation in this secular age.

Redefining Church and Missions in a Secular Age

In a secular age many Christians and churches find themselves building barriers rather than bridges to the nonChristian world. Some of this is unconscious and some is conscious. Some is motivated by fear and some of the actions are motivated by ignorance. The scriptural framework for this manuscript is found in Romans 12:1-2: "Be not conformed to this world, but be ye transformed by the renewing of your mind that you may prove what is that good and acceptable and perfect will of God." Certainly we are not to embrace the secular ideals of the world, but we are to learn to embrace the world — remember Jesus came to die for the world! The first section of this book seeks to help us reframe some aspects of our church and personal ministry in ways that are more effective in an unchurched culture. Not to compromise the Good News, but to discover more effective ways to communicate it. That was Paul's challenge as he ministered among the Roman and Gentile worlds. Tom Sine, in his powerful book *Mustard Seed Vs. McWorld: Reinventing Life and Faith for the Future*, declares:

> In the Book of Acts, the church, that first alien community, wasn't a building to go to once a week. It was much more a living, breathing community that was "breaking bread from house to house."
> . . . I'm convinced that the first call of the gospel isn't to proclamation — and I am committed to evangelism. And I don't believe the first call of the gospel is to social action — and I am concerned for the poor. I believe that the first call of the gospel

is to incarnation. Only as we flesh out in community something of the right side-up values of God's new order do we have any basis on which to speak or act.[3]

Paul's world was changing and so is ours.

The Postmodern Church

Yes, our playing field has changed and most churches don't know it or they choose to deny it. Such represents my personal pilgrimage. In many ways I feel fortunate that I grew up for the most part in a church culture environment where most people in my personal world had favorable thoughts, feelings and actions towards the faith system of my family. I grew up in a small cotton mill village church in Greenville, SC. A tight knit community, most worked together, played together and worshiped together. We were predominately a white community with only a few African Americans beginning to move in. That's what appeared to be the fortunate side.

Now for the unfortunate aspects of growing up in that environment. I've spent more than 25 years unlearning much of what I learned in that small prejudiced community. The world I'm seeking to minister to and in, is very different from that small community. My world is best described as multicultural, multiethnic, with growing pluralistic belief systems, increasingly secular and most people without favorable feelings about Christianity and local churches. The blue laws are gone, which prevented us from shopping on Sundays and encouraged our church attendance. Now we're in a 24/7 world (meaning its active 24 hours a day, seven days a week). People work all kind of hours and every day of every week. Competition for people's attention and loyalties are rampant. Mindsets are changing, values are diversifying, and in many cases they are changing. Even those in churches today bring with them a spectrum of values, traditions, cultures and expectations that are outgrowths of our culture. Such diversity in leadership and the pew creates tensions and struggles most churches have never known.

Bill Easum explains, "The modern world took a cognitive approach to discipleship, beginning with belief, moving to belonging, and resulting in behaving. Today's experiential culture requests just the opposite. Discipleship moves from changing one's behavior, to becoming part of a community of friends, to belief in the God seen in those new friends' lives. The day of walking the aisle for Jesus is disappearing in the Western world."4

It's not uncommon for traditional church leaders, who grew up in the world I did to function out of a more modern set of values and mindset that are postmodern. I can hear many of you say — we are supposed to have different values. That is correct. We are not talking about compromising the Holy Scriptures, we are talking how we communicate and work with the secular culture we are now in. What is currently happening in so many churches is that modern minded persons from a traditional church culture are calling the shots — making the decisions — allocating the money — employing the staff — designing our structures and programs. The consequence seems to be that the church is fast becoming irrelevant to the world in which we find ourselves. We are moving from mission mode to a maintenance mode, from mission to survival and now the real challenge we have is outgrowing our ingrown churches.

Church leaders do not like to look at these issues. Many get defensive and push themselves deeper into denial by claiming that the unchurched must meet us (the church culture) halfway. I recently heard several deacons of a large church declare, "I'm getting tired of hearing that those unchurched in our community do not feel welcome or attracted to our church — we're good people, we have good programs, we have good worship...." He didn't hear or understand. The church after all was created by God for those outside its walls, not those of us on the inside. Our mission is not pastoral care, it's "going into all the world and as we go, teach, preach, and baptize."

Indeed the "fields are white unto harvest...and the laborers are indeed few." What does the "playing field" — our mission field — look like these days? Ray Bakke summarizes our new world better than any I know. Look at the realities he uncovers for us — these are shifts in the world we cannot ignore.

• South is coming north, east is coming west, and on all six continents people are migrating to the city.

- In 1900, 8 percent of the world's population lived in cities. Today over 50 percent live in cities.
- There are more Muslims in the cities of the U. K. than there are Baptist and Methodists combined.
- Churches are being recycled — many are now mosques or Sikh temples.
- More than one million Japanese now live in San Palo, Brazil, 80 million Chinese live outside of China. (The largest Chinese school is in Mexico!)
- The sheer pluralism of all these nations are now living in a confined space in cities.

Bakke declares, "mission — as it gets closer to mid-America — is forcing us to reinvent the church and rethink theology." Unfortunately, our seminaries are autobiographical, preparing people to move into the narrow stream of whiteness and middle class. Eighty-seven percent of the world's population is nonwhite. He goes on to report, "I thought the barriers to mission were the big, big cities. But 90 percent of the barriers to reaching the cities are not in the city at all; they are inside our churches. The barriers are inside our structures; the knowledge base, the intimidation factors of our churches." He concludes by explaining, "Mission is no longer about crossing the oceans, jungles and deserts, but about crossing the streets of the world's cities."5

When you look at the families in this pluralistic and changing world it again screams of change:

- In 1979, 71 percent of US households were nuclear families (biologically connected families).
- In 1999, 26 percent of US households were nuclear families.
- Blended families, mixed marriages, cohabitation and multiracial and multicultural families are increasing at exponential rates.
- Single parent families and step-families are increasing.

The playing field has changed! However most churches haven't changed in decades — and most take great comfort and pride in that fact. Somehow we have convinced ourselves as Christian leaders that not changing our methods, structures, worship styles and times is part of our faithfulness. Again let me say, I'm not suggesting that we change our message or compromise the Good News. I'm declaring a truth of church history. Our methods and strategies and even our language has to change if we are to be faithful and effective in reaching our changing culture.

Maybe we should consider some of the following concepts as we fashion an effective ministry in the early decades of the twenty-first century. How we define these words concepts are critical. We must realize we are speaking to a very diverse group, coming to spiritual formation from many different value systems and belief systems and church backgrounds. There are those of us who grew up in a church culture, and have been involved in church — comfortable with all the traditional language and programs. Then there are those who grew up in a church culture, but had a bad experience for what ever reason and resist the language (that often brings flashbacks of pain) but they embrace the principles. Then there are those from other belief systems/religions and those from other cultures. How do we communicate the truth to them? How do we build bridges of faith formation to them rather than erect barriers to their pursuit of the God of truth and the healing and hope God provides?

While these terms may not connect with many church culture people, they do represent some of the aspirations of many who are seeking and searching for God, for truth, for healing, for hope. In light of this changing landscape of ministry how can we communicate effectively the Gospel of Christ in ways that this multicultural, pluralistic, and diverse world can not only hear, but also respond to the message? How do you take someone who is from a secular, postmodern culture and grow him or her forward in faith? How do you attract them? Assimilate them? Disciple them? Deploy them?

Leonard Sweet, a prolific author and professor at Drew Divinity School, contributes much to help us wrestle with the modern and postmodern issues and the pathways to effective ministry in this new world. Some of his most helpful works include "Soul Tsunami," "Aqua Church," "Soul Salsa," and his ever-changing and challenging website www.leonardsweet.com. I heard him explain his EPIC theory several years ago and it has been a guide for me in practical ministry and the formation of this book:

E — Experiential
P — Participatory
I — Image rich
C — Connector[6]

Sweet challenges us to evaluate all our programming, ministries and efforts at being church in this postmodern world using EPIC. In the modern world much of what the church focused on was rational faith; now we must create experiences to facilitate faith and community. In the modern world performance captured many church agendas. In a postmodern culture we should focus on participation. Then a major shift for many is moving from a verbal or word orientation to communication to images. Finally he suggests moving from an individual focus to connecting persons with each other and with God. These are the issues we'll wrestle with in the remainder of this book.

Reframing Hints To Ponder

- In a secular age many Christians and churches find themselves building barriers rather than bridges to the non-Christian world.
- Only as we flesh out in community something of the right side-up values of God's new order do we have any basis on which to speak or act.
- Our playing field has changed and most churches don't know it or they choose to deny it.
- We are now in a postmodern and secular culture rather than a churched culture.
- The church was created by God for those outside its walls not those of us on the inside.
- Our mission is not pastoral care, it is "going into all the world and as we go teach, preach, and baptize."
- Mission is forcing us to reinvent the church and rethink theology.

Common Questions Today's Leaders Ask About Christian Education

When I graduated from seminary in the early 1980s and went to my first church as Minister in Education the questions I was asking and that our congregation was asking were very different than the questions I am hearing and wrestling with as we enter the twenty-first century. In the '80s many of our questions and most of our meetings were to take care of us, to make us feel better, to help us be more knowledgeable of the Bible, and to be better churchgoers. There were very few serious conversations about the changing community we were in, the growing diversity of people groups moving into our neighborhood (for it was only beginning during those days).

Today, those churches wanting to be faithful to the Great Commission in a secular culture are being challenged with a whole new set of questions and facing major shifts in their communities and consequentially their value systems. Traditionalists are struggling with how to preserve the integrity of the scripture, as they have experienced it, amidst the rapidly changing world they now find themselves in. Churches that have been institutionally based desire to maintain and preserve that which they've known and have benefited from while those in the next generation have little interest in or value for those same traditions. What now? Different questions are being forced and many leaders, programs and organizations are in crisis. Let's simply review some of the prevalent questions being asked by some, struggled with by others and avoided or intentionally ignored by most of our existing church leadership:

• How do we reach others while keeping the existing members?
• How do we do Christian education in light of the pluralistic culture in which we are living?
• How do we do Christian education for the 5 to 6 generations that are inside most churches? Considering different learning styles, preferences of worship styles, etc.?
• How do we reach, guide and assist the spiritual formation of those in the churched and the unchurched culture?

- How do we select effective curricula/literature for the diversity within our church and community?
- How do we revise our organizational structure to maintain what is and facilitate the mission of the church?
- How do we refocus the leaders of our congregation and move them toward greater effectiveness in our rapidly changing culture?
- How can what we do in Christian education more effectively impact daily life for the cause of Christ?
- What is the impact of technology on the way we do spiritual formation?

These and many other questions are direct consequences of some or all of many of the transitions summarized in the chart below. While I'm sure they are generalizations and represent a continuum for most churches rather than a direct impact, these shifts are worthy of consideration. However, the more extreme and multiple the shifts are in any given program or organization the more likely the tensions created by imbalance and/or growing ineffectiveness.

Shifts Emerging In Traditional Forms of Christian Education

FROM	TO
Programs	Process/Spiritual Formation
Printed Literature	Life Curricula
Print	Technology
Institution Focus	Life Need Focus
Committees	Teams
Teachers	Facilitation or Team Teaching
Pastor/staff led	Lay Led Ministries
Bible Knowledge	Theological Reflection & Storytelling
Human Development Organization	Spiritual Formation Sensitivity
Just Age Graded	Affinity Group Organization
Just a church culture focus	Pluralistic Culture Sensitivity
Single track	Multiple & Diverse track for spiritual formation
Church Base	Community Partnerships
Just core relationships	Virtual relationships and accountability
Membership	Meaningfulness
Cognitive exercises	Relational, hands on experiences
Time and building limitations	Convenience and comfort challenges
Segregated programming and curricula	Integrated and intergenerational experiences
Collective gatherings	Affinity focused communities
Community standards	Comfortable entry points
Just print & verbal	Visual and metaphorical
Giving answers	Finding the "right questions"
Followership	Mutual leadership
Church ministry	Lay ministry

Discovering Effective Measurements
for What Matters in a Secular Age

How many of these shifts have already occurred in your congregation? How many of them are points of tension for your leaders? For your participants? Take the time and mark appropriate responses with differing color of pens for those in each category mentioned here.

It's not unusual in my work with churches of various types and sizes to discover that leaders have a different opinion or experience with these issues than the participants in their congregation. Also, it's not unusual for the clergy and laity to have differing opinions or experiences. Such discrepancy frequently creates tension that is not recognized and often not discussed. Consequently the tensions and discrepancies increase. Very often these tensions are epitomized by the real struggle found in "managing the present while preparing for the future" of the congregation or church based program traditions.

The questions people are asking, out of the tensions they are experiencing in life, often serve as avenues for new measuring sticks for helping move persons forward in their spiritual walk. For instance if they are needing to deal with prejudices bias toward multicultural issues, the role of spiritual leaders is to ask how can we help move them forward in their journey in a way that preserves and builds Kingdom integrity. In a church culture we measured our church based programs on how many persons came to them and how much money persons gave who participated. Now that we are in a secular culture we have to learn to measure things that matter to Christ in this culture that can contribute to God's Kingdom's purposes. Such is certainly a struggle for most church persons, but in many circumstances if we

---

Reframing Hints To Ponder

- Traditionalists are struggling with how to preserve the integrity of scripture, as they have experienced it, amidst the rapidly changing world they now find themselves in

- Churches that have been institutionally based desire to maintain and preserve that which they have known and have benefited from while those in the next generation have little interest in or value for those same traditions.

- How do we reach others while keeping the existing members?

listen carefully to the seekers and searchers they can help us reframe new goals, objectives and standards for a ministry that would reach and keep them. Learning such listening skills and finding the faith to take the needed risks may be the greatest challenge here for most church leadership.

Mobilizing the Church for Effective Ministry in the Twenty-First Century

During these days of extreme change and transition we need to remember the church is to be more of a living dynamic organism than a static organization from which people desire something. Many seem to go to church for what the church can offer them rather than what the church represents. In the last decades of the churched culture many Christians joined churches for what the church could give their families — better programming and pastoral care were the attractions of the day. As we enter the twenty-first century and learn to be relevant and functional in a secular, unchurched and postmodern culture, the church has to remember again "God so loved the *world* that He *gave* . . ." The Word becoming flesh was the essence of New Testament Christianity. What are the ways the church of the twenty-first century can become a participatory body rather than a group of spectators? How can the Body of Christ become an active, viable and ever present force within the secular culture? What are the implications of these issues for the clergy and the laity in leadership in today's churches?

Believers — Participators or Spectators?

The church I grew up in and which nurtured me taught me, and many others to be good "church members." Persons who would "come to" church programs, "serve on" church committees and busy themselves with "church work." We learned this lesson well. So well, that now my home church and many of the churches I encounter across this country, are self-absorbed and so ingrown that the Great Commission seems lost or minimized to a seasonal mission offering. In some ways the fact that we have become such good "churchpersons" has helped create the secular paganistic world in which we live. Pogo says it best, "We have met the enemy and he is us."

The twenty-first century is calling us back to the realities of the early church we learn of in the Book of Acts and reminds us of the mandate to "Go into all the world and make disciples...." The church age taught us to "come to the church" and to "serve in the church" and to "take care of the church people." Now God calls loudly, through the lostness of our world and the pains of our nation. He is calling for us to "*Go into* all the world," and to "*serve in the world* as salt, light and leaven" and to "*minister to those in the world* who are hurt, broken, blind and in bondage." and to be about the work of the church. (John 3:16, Matt 25)

No longer can we simply follow our comfortable traditions of calling paid staff to do the work of ministry. Scripture is clear that the clergy are the "equippers of the Saints (all the people of God) for ministry" (Eph 4, 1 Pet 2:9). The ministry belongs to *all* Believers. The secular culture of the twenty-first century is demanding that we "learn to reap the harvest while it is yet in the fields." People will come to church after they have experienced authentic relationships with those in their neighborhoods, workplaces or community clubs.

Membership in most churches during the last 50 plus years hinged upon a person's commitment to occasional attendance, minimal participation in church programs and optional service and giving. Such membership standards have created for the most part an apathetic, poorly disciplined, spiritually shallow, biblically illiterate, morally dissolving membership that is more self-absorbed than servant postured.

Ray Bakke understands the fragile state of the church in this pluralistic secular culture when he declares that, "City pastors must be missiologically trained. We would never think of sending a person to a people group without language and cultural study. Urban neighborhoods are more complex than tribal cultures." Bakke further reveals, "I thought the barriers to mission were the big, big cities. But 90 percent of the barriers to reaching the cities are not in the city at all; they are inside our churches. The barriers are inside our structures: the knowledge base, the intimidation factors of our churches."7

With such realities and weakening membership, it is little wonder that there is an increasingly secularization of our culture. When good people do nothing, evil takes root and grows.

Becoming the Scattered Church

Loren Mead reminds us, "Through the centuries 'gathered and scattered' has become a description not of two different actions, but of the one vital, continuing double-movement of the people of God. It is but one movement, the gathering and the scattering. No issue troubles Christian leaders more than finding how to bring to life the New Testament image of the church gathering itself in order to propel its people outward to the world, driven by the gospel into a life of service in the world."[8]

One of the most significant challenges the church faces as we enter the twenty-first century is redefining success and effectiveness in ministry. For in the last decades our success was based on how many people came to our church buildings for our church programs. As long as the pews and programs were full and the budget was being met or exceeded, then ministers and churches were seen as successful. However in the secular culture of the twenty-first century church the way we evaluate our effectiveness and success will have to change. If we are going to turn the church around and move from apathy to action, from spectators to participants in the mission, we must align ourselves, our goals, our standards with those of the New Testament church, those set out in scripture within the context of the realities of our culture and age. (In *The Gathered and Scattered Church* I've dealt with this extensively.)

For illustration purposes let me challenge you to explore some of these assessment questions and then to explore them with some of your leaders.

Evaluating Effectiveness in Ministry
Outreach Efforts to Unchurched and Under–churched Persons

- How much time and encouragement (permission) do we provide to the church members to enable them to cultivate or reach out to the unchurched?
- What are the limits we place on the amount of time church people give to ministering to those inside the church verses the amount of expectation and time we place upon their ministry to the unchurched world?

Assimilation

- How intentional are we about involving prospects, attendees and/or new members into our established church activities? (How do they know they are invited? Who has this responsibility? How are they mentored through this experience?)
- How intentional are we about assessing the giftedness, calling and needs of our attendees, new members and prospects? (Who has this responsibility? What is done with the gathered information?)
- How many new persons have been assimilated into our leadership base, committees, workgroups, small groups, etc.?

Fellowship Involvement

- How many fellowship groups (fishing pools — comfortable non-threatening entry points) have been created this year in each Sunday School department, music ministry etc.?
- How many connections have we nurtured/encouraged/facilitated among various groupings within the congregation and community? (i.e. vocational groupings like affinity groups; persons in same community, who attend the same school; etc.)[3]

Mobilizing Laity in Ministry

Raising the bar of expectation is a must. All believers, all church members face the biblical mandate to "be priests" (1 Pet 2:9-10) and to "be salt, light and leaven." Moving a congregation's expectations from that of "spectator to participant," from "pew sitter to priest," from "manager of programs to minister in the world" will take time, patience, and skills leadership. A basic principle will be change values before you change behaviors and structures.

It will be critical that sermons be preached, lessons to be taught, articles be written in church newsletters, testimonies be shared, books be available and read, dialogues be experienced, affirmations and challenges be voiced and then do it all over again and again if values are to be changed. It will be essential that intentional efforts be made at accountability, gift discovery, and discernment of calling. (See resource list at end of chapter for suggestions to help in each of these areas of ministry.)

Reframing Hints To Ponder

- During these days of extreme change and transition we need to remember the church is to be more of a living dynamic organism than a static organization from which people desire something.
- The Word becoming flesh was the essence of New Testament Christianity.
- No longer can we simply follow our comfortable traditions of calling paid professional staff to do the work of ministry.
- The ministry belongs to ALL the people of God.
- One of the most significant challenges the church faces as we enter the twenty-first century is redefining success and effectiveness in ministry.
- Change values before you change structures.
- It will be essential that intentional efforts be made at accountability, gift discovery, and discernment of calling.

What the Church Is Not Talking About

In recent days our state convention staff has been intentional about updating our understanding of the state and world we are living in and in which we are called to minister. We've been privileged to dialogue with many state government, academic institutions and denominational leaders who are specialists in the areas of multicultural studies, sociological and demographic trends. As I work to digest the content of these presentations over the last eight months or so, it seems fairly clear to me that most of our church leaders are not talking about many of the issues that these leaders see as current or imminent for our ministry focus. Permit me to share very succinct summaries of some of the issues I'm working with in a new light. I suggest using this as a checklist with your leadership. How often do these issues surface in your meetings, planning, prayer life? How often are they encountered in daily life, but not intentionally brought to church life and planning?

Surfacing the Vital Issues We Frequently Overlook

One of our major objectives as a state convention staff is to refashion ourselves as a learning organization. That is to be a team-based organization that works from our strengths, callings and passion and to collaborate with others to insure our training is informed by the most current, relevant information possible. Whereas in the past we were basically a training organization designed to assist churches with church programs, today, because of the rapid rate of change and the topics I will summarize here, we are moving to become not just a training organization, but a learning organization. This will help insure that our training, planning and modeling will be in keeping with the best information available to help churches and her leaders to move toward greater health and effectiveness in their ministry. Here are some of the vital issues many are overlooking:

• *Population and demographic shifts are all around us.* We are learning that when those from the north move to the south new challenges, cultures and needs surface. Also, the graying of America continues, while there is a rise in the number of children and youth. However, many of those are from single parent or no parent families, with few, if any, of their extended family around them.

The population shifts are creating many challenges. For now most communities have four or five different generations present for the first time in our history. People are living longer and are healthier. Such diversity is certain to surface generation gaps in styles, preferences of music, preaching, etc. It also surfaces challenges among leadership and the way they make decisions about the mission of the church or the way it is accomplished.

• *Economic shifts are everywhere.* The aged population is basically carrying the economic demands of our churches. They are faithful, consistent and committed to tithing and cooperative missions giving. The younger boomer, buster, and Generation X persons are not as educated, committed or faithful to these traditional principles. Some of the reason is they haven't been taught about tithing, but in large part their values are different. They want to be involved in missions and not just give money to missions. Frequently, when they are involved they give in excess. Much tension is often created in a church when the "purse strings" are held by those from the depression years and leadership is not representative of all generations seeking to work toward consensus. Another learning is that women are fast becoming the primary economic base in the world.

We are also learning that the middle class is fading away. The "haves" and the "have nots" are the two basic realities in our culture. Frequently our ministry objectives focus on one of the groups over another.

• *Multiculturalism is here to stay.* People groups from all over the world have come to the shores of America. People with different languages, belief systems, world views, understandings of God, cultural traditions concerning holidays, family, economics, and education . . . Some churches seem to be ignoring this reality or pretending it will eventually go away by their silence or arguing to return to the "good old days," or that these outside groups should just do things "our way." This reality and struggle is here to stay. The mission field and other religions' missionaries are now here evangelizing your community and mine.

In North Carolina we are currently worshiping in 24 languages every week. We are involved in 197 ethnic congregations and are working strategically to start new work among other groups all across this state. Could you help? Give? Go?

• *Shifts in the job world abound,* but the church again doesn't seem to be intentionally working with these realities. The 24–hour world is here. Stores are open for business around the clock, therefore our people are having to work various hours and we still content that the Sunday Morning time for church is THE time we will offer Bible study, worship and fellowship. Many say, "if they really loved Jesus they would come on Sunday." Who then will staff our hospitals, fire and police departments and the restaurants you and I go to after worship?

The realities are the dual career households, people working from home, women in the work world, etc. What are churches doing to help these realities have a God-focus and a Kingdom objective?

• *The unclear lines between the churched and the unchurched are real.* Not only do the unchurched persons outnumber the churched, but in the day to day world it is increasingly difficult to tell those who attend church from those who do not. Currently the divorce rate among Christians is higher than the divorce rate of the unchurched. Ethical behaviors and attitudes of the churched are rarely discernibly different from the unchurched.

• *The changing nature of the family is also all around us.* People are separated from biological families due to career or choice and are creating surrogate families among friends, colleagues, work associates and community members. Persons are living together out of wedlock due to various economic and personal realities. Children are from blended families, multicultural relationships and a host of varying belief systems, traditions and family schedules. Does your family night include these people groups? Do you want them to "be like you/us" or are you customizing and recognizing their uniqueness and meeting them where they are, rather than where we would choose them to be. Seems like Jesus had counsel for this in his encounter with the woman at the well.

• *The high tech world is changing our world rapidly.* Because of the internet there is an information explosion. Most of our preschoolers and children know more about computers than their parents and certainly their grandparents. However, because of technology we have instant communication. Letter writing has given way to email and now we get the latest information in real time on the web. We can order our groceries or visit our bank or doctor without ever leaving our home. Computer technology is now driving curricula design, learning environments and opportunities via teleconferencing, phone bridges and on-line seminars. New communities and relationships are being developed in cyberspace. Such technology is heightening our level of expectations about all printed materials and educational forums. Does your church still use a mimeograph machine or just a one-color printer? Are your records on computer or on paper? These issues make loud statements to persons from the high-tech world that visits your congregation. Are you sending a message of hope for the future or of being bound to the past?

Well, how are you doing personally with these realities? What about your Sunday School class or discipleship group? What about your deacons and church leadership? How might you introduce these to church leaders for an intentional time of prayer, study, and planning? Do you want to "Go ye into all the world..." or do you just prefer to live in the world you create and are comfortable with?

We are all being called and challenged anew to remember that Jesus died for the world and not just for the church and that there is no comfort on the cross. We have lived in our comfort zones far to long. Now we are challenged to confront and deal with stark realities. If we choose not to work with these realities we are probably deciding for the erosion of our church in the years ahead — for the world in 2020 will not be the world of today! The Gospel will not and should not be compromised, but the methodology and leadership style is to be adjusted.

Now that we've explored some of the reasons to reframe discipleship, let's look at the practical challenges we will likely encounter as we seek to improve the relevancy and impact of the church in today's and tomorrow's increasingly secular world.

Reframing Hints To Ponder

- Population shifts are creating many new challenges.
- As the aged population, who currently provides basis of our financial and leadership support, dies out the church faces a serious crisis.
- Multiculturalism is here to stay, but churches are not ready.
- Shifts in the job world are occurring but the church is not responding.
- Lines between the churched and unchurched are blurring.
- The nature of the family is changing, but the church is not responding.
- Technology is changing our world, but having a tough time breaking into most churches.

Notes

[1] Randy Frazee, *The Connecting Church: Beyond Small Groups to Authentic Community* (Grand Rapids MI: Zondervan, 2001), 37.

[2] Julie Kay, "Barna: Churches Must Change," *The Advocate Online* (21 April 2001).

[3] Tom Sine, *Mustard Seed Vs. McWorld: Reinventing Life and Faith for the Future* (Minneapolis MN: Baker Books, 1999), 205.

[4] Bill Easum, "21st Century Evangelism," *Net Results* (February 2001): 22-23.

[5] Ray Bakke, "Loving Our World," *Reconcilation Magazine* (Summer 2000): 24-25.

[6] Leonard Sweet, *Nashville: Post Modern Pilgrims* (Broadman Holman, 2001).

[7] Ray Bakke, "Loving the Urban World," *Reconciliation Magazine* (Summer 2000): 24.

[8] Loren Mead, "Foreward" in *The Gathered and Scattered Church: Equipping Believers for the 21st Century* by Edward H. Hammett (Macon GA: Smyth & Helwys, 2000), iv.

Resources

Spiritual Gifts

Motivation & Equipment for Effective Ministry
(Suggested Resources for the Individual & Groups)

- *Crossseekers: Gifted! Serving in Christ's Name.* Designed for college students. Inventory included.
- *Discovering God's Vision for Your Life/You and Your Spiritual Gifts* by Kenneth Haugk (Stephens Ministry, 1999).
- *Gifts of Grace: Discovering and Using Your Spiritual Gifts.* Leader's and Member's Guides by Larry Garner and Tony Martin (Nelson Pucket Press, 1995).
- *Developing Deacon Ministry Teams: Meeting Needs Through Discovering and Using Spiritual Gifts* by Larry Garner, John Temple, Keith Wilkinson (Deacon Ministry Dynamics, 1997).
- *Serving God: Discovering and Using Your Spiritual Gifts.* Ken Hemphill (Sampson Press, 1995). Video and Interactive Workbooks. Designed for six 40-55 minute sessions.

Testing Instruments/Gift Studies

- *Discovering My Ministry: A Workbook* by Harry C. Griffith (Adventures in Ministry).
- *Team Ministry Spiritual Gifts Inventory Questionnaire* (Church Growth Institute).
- *Discover Your Gifts Workbook* (Christian Reformed Home Missions).
- *Unleash Your Church: A Comprehensive Strategy to Help People Discover and Use Their Spiritual Gifts* by Paul Ford (Fuller Institute, 1994).
- *Spiritual Gifts, One Spirit, Many Gifts* by Patricia D. Brown (Abingdon, 1996). Includes an inventory, gift description and discovery exercises.
- *Network* by Bruce Bugbee, Don Cousins, Bill Hybels (Zondervan, 1994). Includes video, workbooks, implementation guide, overhead masters.

Book Resources

- Allen, Lloyd. *Gift Quest— A Search for Spiritual Gifts.* Birmingham, AL: World Changers Resources, 1993. (Resource for Youth)
- Bauknight, Brian K. *Body Building: Creating a Ministry Team Through Spiritual Gifts.* Cokesbury, 1995.
- Bryant, Charles. *Rediscovering Our Spiritual Gifts.* Upper Room Publishing, 1991.
- Bugbee, Bruce. *What You Do Best in the Body of Christ—Discover Your Spiritual Gifts, Personal Style and God Given Passions.* Zondervan, 1996.
- Calvert, Stuart. *Uniquely Gifted- Discovering Your Spiritual Gifts.* New Hope Publisher, 1993.
- Carter, William. *Team Spirituality: A Guide for Church and Staff.* Abingdon Press, 1998.
- Edwards, Lloyd. *Discerning Your Spiritual Gifts.* Cowley Publication, 1988.
- Gilbert, Larry. *Team Ministry—A Guide to Spiritual Gifts and Lay Involvement.* Lynchburg, VA: Church Growth Institute, 1999.
- Hammett, Edward H. *The Gathered and Scattered Church: Equipping Believers for the 21st Century.* Smyth and Helwys, 2000.
- _____. *Making the Church Work: Converting the Church for the 21st Century.* Smyth & Helwys, 1997.

29

- Harbaugh, Gary. *God's Gifted People*. Augsburg Press, 1990.
- Hemphill, Kenneth. *Mirror Mirror On the Wall - Discovering Yourself Through Spiritual Gifts*. Broadman Press, 1992.
- _____. *Spiritual Gifts Empowering the New Testament Church*. Broadman Press, 1988.
- McMakin, Jacqueline. *Doorways to Christian Growth*. Harper and Row, 1984.
- Ware, Corinne. *Discover Your Spiritual Type: A Guide to Individual and Congregational Growth*. Alban Institute, 1996.

Church Membership
Book Resources

- Blue, Ken and John White. *Church Discipline that Heals*. InterVarsity Press, 1995
- Easum, Bill. *Growing Spiritual Redwood*. Abingdon, 1999.
- Edge, Findley. *Quest for Vitality in Religion*. Smyth and Helwys, 1997.
- Friedman, Matt. *The Accountability Connection*. Victor Press, 1992.
- Hammett, Edward. *The Gathered and Scattered Church: Equipping Believers for the 21st Century*. Smyth and Helwys, 1999.
- Klaas, Alan. *In Search of the Unchurched: Why People Don't Join your Congregation*. Alban Institute, 1998.
- Malphurs, Aubrey. *Pouring New Wine into Old Wineskins*. Baker, 1993.
- Mead, Loren. *Transforming Congregations for the Future*. Alban Institute, 1998.
- Ogden, Greg. *The New Reformation*. Zondervan, 1991.
- Oswald, Roy. *Making Your Church More Inviting*. Alban Institute, 1998.
- Roehlkepartain, Eugene. *The Teaching Church — Moving Christian Education to Center Stage*. Abingdon Press, 1993.
- Southerland, Dan. *Transitioning*. Serendipity House, 1999.
- Warren, Rick. *The Purpose Driven Church*. Zondervan, 1995.

Journals and Magazines

- Bandy, Thomas. "Seeking Out Seekers: Choosing The Right Time," *Net Results*, (November 1999): 17.
- Easum, William. "The Blurring of Infant and Adult Baptism," *Net Results*, (November 1999): 22-24.
- Foss, Mike. "No More Members, Moving From Membership to Discipleship," *Rev. Magazine* (July and August 2000).
- Johnson, Erik. "How to Be An Effective Mentor: Making Devoted Disciples," *Leadership Journal* (Spring 2000) 36-42.
- Thomas, Frank. "New Members Boot Camp: Entry Level Experience Starts Everyone Off as a Disciple," *Leadership Journal* (Spring 2000): 34-36.

Challenges to Reframing

Outgrowing an Ingrown Church

The urgency about reframing is captured by Tom Sine as he shares these sobering remarks about the Western Church:

> As we look into the future, we are witnessing the incredible shrinking Western Church. And within two decades the Western church is likely to see even more rapid decline because of our inability to reach and keep the young. It is my reluctant conclusion that unless something dramatic happens to change the present trends, the church is not only likely to become significantly smaller in the first two decades of the twenty-first century; it will also have significantly less time and resources to invest in mission world to meet the growing needs likely to fill tomorrow's world.[1]

There are many spiritually thirsty people in our land, but few of them are going to churches to quench that thirst. Instead they are seeking answers to life's questions and searches for meaning through a variety of sources and relationships. Why are they not going to the churches for help? Many of them will say they are not going because they have already been and didn't find authenticity or relevant help in days gone by. Others will tell you that the church is not on a quest for truth, but simply another political organization. Still others will tell you that the church is little less than a "country club" for persons they want to be members and all others find it very difficult to get in. Such an ingrown nature is what we are talking about here.

A prevalent reality of our age is the ingrown nature of many churches. These are churches that are so inwardly focused that they cannot be effective in going into all the world to spread the Good News. Churches seem to have lost sight of their biblical mission and have become content on taking care of those who are active members. In fact, many churches and church leaders seem to believe their mission is that of caring for its members. While this is a vital role of church, it is *not* the biblical mission. How do we help ingrown churches turn their focus from themselves to reaching and ministering to the lost, hurting, and needy as mandated in the scriptures? (Isa 61, Matt 28, Acts 2)

Recognizing An Ingrown Church

Ingrown churches seem to exhibit various characteristics. While many might consider these characteristics good, frequently they fuel an ingrown, maintenance-minded congregation.

Characteristics include:

- Focus on those inside the church rather than those outside.
- More time spent taking care of "us," rather than reaching "them."
- Finances go toward maintaining buildings and membership rather than reaching and ministering to those outside the church.
- Program and ministry planning seem to focus on those in attendance rather than those we are called to reach.
- Leadership core seems preoccupied with care-giving rather than evangelism and missions.
- Church business meetings focused more on pampering the membership than evangelizing the world.

While these are only indicative, they are not exhaustive. An ingrown state has more to do with a mindset and core values of a congregation than just various administrative details.

It is amazing to me the number of church members I encounter who believe that the church exists to take care of those who are members — those who are inside the walls and far too often those who are active in attendance. Pastoral care of the membership seems to be the focus of much of the activity, dialogue, and planning. In fact pastoral care of the membership seems to be a primary criterion for evaluating the success and effectiveness of the leadership — clergy and laity. While this seems to be a popular mindset for many churches, the scriptures are very clear that the primary purpose of the church is to "Go into all the world . . . as you go teach, preach and baptize . . . " (Matt 28:19-20 paraphrase). It is also clear that Jesus, our primary role model for Christianity, spent more time with the sinners than he did in church meetings. He spent more time on reaching the poor, lame and sick than he spent with the wealthy and healthy. How did we become so ingrown?

Mirroring Reality in an Ingrown Church

Leading in an ingrown church is often filled with "warm fuzzies" for those leaders (clergy and laity alike) who are great caregivers — leaders who visit regularly and nurture the hurting and needy of the congregation. They visit hospitals, perform or attend weddings and funerals, make house visits, and pay close attention to members present at church gatherings. However, these leaders are often not leading the church into the future; instead they are enabling the church to turn inward and in most cases planting the seeds of death for the congregation. While these caregiving leaders are doing a great and needed ministry to those in need inside the congregation, they are not leading the church to accomplish the biblical mission and please our God. Now, lest I be misunderstood. I'm not against good pastoral care of the flock. I am against that being assumed to be *the* biblical mission of the church.

Clarifying the biblical mission of the church and aligning our congregational values to that biblical mission is a real challenge in many churches. Until we face such reality and come to the place of making needed adjustments, reaching out to the unchurched, secular minded population is unlikely in most situations. Lyle Schaller, the pioneering church consultant for decades, provides a great tool for mirroring realities of a congregation potentially positioning themselves for decline. Evaluate your congregation using his signals for a plateauing congregation.

What Are the Signals?

What are the signals that suggest the numerically growing congregation is about to drift off onto a plateau in size or begin to experience a decline in numbers?

- Taking better care of today's members moves ahead of evangelism and outreach to the unchurched on the local list of priorities.
- The pastor spends more time thinking and talking about retirement a few years hence than devoting himself or herself to outreach and evangelism. A parallel signal often begins to flash when the number one issue on the current agenda is the resolution of conflict.
- The average attendance at worship begins to drop when compared to the same months a year earlier.
- The average attendance in Sunday School begins to decline.
- The unhappy or involuntary termination of two consecutive pastors often is followed by a plateau of decline in numbers. A parallel signal is a succession of two to four year pastorates.
- The key signal often is a decrease in the number of households that underwrite most of the annual budget.
- A decline in the number of new members received by letter or transfer of certificate from other churches.
- When the total compensation of the paid staff exceeds 50 percent of the total member contributions.
- When references to the past begin to overshadow plans, dreams, and hope for the future of the congregation.
- A decrease in the number of baptisms.
- When the new minister spends more time with individuals than with groups of people.
- A decline in the net worth of all capital assets (land, building, cash reserves, investments), after full adjustments for inflation and depreciation, often is a signal.
- If at least half of today's members joined more than 10 years earlier.
- If, week after week, nearly everyone has disappeared within 10 to 12 minutes after the benediction at the close of the last Sunday morning worship service.
- Cutting back on special worship services (Thanksgiving, Christmas Eve, Holy Week, special anniversaries, etc.).

- A drop in the total dollars given for missions and benevolences.
- An inability to design and implement a five-year plan for ministry, program and outreach.
- A decrease in the proportion of teenagers from outside the membership who are regularly involved in youth ministries.
- Seniority, tenure, and kinship or friendship ties with members of the nominating committee often outweigh skill, wisdom, creativity, competence, experience in other congregations, or enthusiasm in choosing policy makers for the coming year.
- The ratio of worship attendance to membership drops year after year.
- The response to an impending financial problem is to concentrate on reducing expenditures rather than on increasing dollar receipts.
- The only significant increase in total receipts year after year is in rentals received for use of the real estate or in the size of the denominational subsidy or in income from the endowment fund.
- A rise in the median age is often a sign of future numerical decline. The decision to cut back on programming, the Sunday morning schedule, staff, finances, weekday programming, outreach, benevolences, or office hours is often an early warning sign of future decline.

In other words, for today's numerically growing churches, the best response to the tendency to rest on a comfortable plateau in size is to watch for those early warning signs and initiate preventive action.[2]

Leaders (clergy and laity alike) must help congregations mirror reality and thus come to an understanding and acceptance of the inward mindset and distraction from the biblical mission. Such can be done in several ways:

- Preach and teach regularly on the biblical mission of the church.
- Work diligently and intentionally with deacons and church leaders to help them develop their outward focus.
- Ask the hard questions when it comes to planning and budgeting meetings. Are we taking care of ourselves or trying to reach the unreached?

- Work with your congregation to rethink your definitions of success. (See my *The Gathered and Scattered Church*.)
- When leaders begin to refocus the church, or try to refocus the church, recognize that many members will likely be offended that they are no longer in the forefront on your mind. But wherever the leaders lead, whatever model they project, is where the congregation or class is likely to follow. God needs a few leaders who are willin to stand in the gap to help outgrow an ingrown church.[3]

What It Takes to Outgrow an Ingrown Church

Outgrowing an ingrown church takes a clear vision of the biblical purpose of the church, a commitment to focusing on that mission, good planning skills, conflict management skills, patience, prayer, and intentionality. Outgrowing an ingrown church is tough work calling forth the best in leaders. The challenge before lay and clergy leaders include the following steps:

- Assessing the situation.
- Revisiting the biblical mandate for the church.
- Rethinking the definition of success for programs, budgeting and ministries.
- Focused prayer on persons, issues, and groups needing to refocus.
- Courage to take risks in relationships and leadership among their peers.
- Dependency upon the leadership of the Holy Spirit.
- Working patiently, but deliberately with the most open groups to help them model this transition.
- Sensitivity to the feelings of persons being faced with a reality that causes them some losses, grief, and readjustment.
- Mirroring realities of discrepancies between biblical mandates and current congregational practices.

The challenge of outgrowing an ingrown church is often overwhelming for Christian leaders. Who wants to take on such an assignment when you know you are going against the tide, the preferences of most of the parishioners, and calling them to a commitment beyond their comfort zones? The leaders who take on this challenge exhibit great courage, commitment, and desire to please God. They also need encouragement, support, and prayer from supportive persons.

Very often an ingrown church is being led not by the Holy Spirit, but by the personal preferences of a small group of leaders who are perceived as the "power group" of the church or by traditions or comfort zones from the past. How do you determine who is leading your church and what do you then do when your church doesn't want to be led?[4]

Part of the challenge for an ingrown church in our secular culture is to shift values from "taking care of us" to "taking care of us and reaching them." Let me suggest several ideas for your consideration as a class, church, family, or individual. I make these suggestions in response to a phrase I often hear from church people — "we can't find any prospects" or "we don't know how to find the spiritually thirsty." These are not theoretical suggestions — they are tried and true from my personal and professional journey of shifting my values from "taking care of us" to "reaching them." Discuss them with your class, family, or church and make plans to try an idea or two and bathe your actions in private and corporate prayer.

How To Find People Interested in Spiritual Things — Pre-Conversion Discipleship

Discern whom God is challenging you to reach. Ask yourself and others:
- Who are the people you naturally intersect with on a regular basis?
- For whom do you feel a burden? What people group pulls at your heartstrings?
- Where are the places in your town that spiritually thirsty people show up or cluster together?
- Movies, radio shows, internet chat rooms, bookstores, cafés, coffee shops, lecture series at the university, Christian concerts, community agencies that serve others, volunteer organizations, etc.
- Do you have persons in your church/group that are connected with some of these "fields ready for cultivating"?
- How can you enlist their help in identifying or cultivating?
- Become intentional about listening to and observing those around you wherever you go. Are they curious about spiritual things? How

might you invite them into a nonthreatening, comfortable conversation/experience with you?

- Is there a way to cluster those discovered persons together in a nonthreatening, comfortable place at a time most convenient for them? (not likely to be Sunday at 10 a.m.). *Remember we meet them where they ARE, not where we desire them to be!*
- Utilize local newspapers, cable shows, and radio stations to identify some of those in the following groups or life situations. Read carefully — crime situations in a community, newborns, crises support groups, death notices, divorce notices, etc.

Seeing Life's Rites of Passage as Open Doors for Discipleship

- Cluster groups after a community tragedy has hit. (tornadoes, youth suicide, etc.)
- Newborns/newlyweds
- Parents in Crises
- Aging parents' groups
- Transitional careers
- Newcomers to a community
- Death & dying situations
- Divorce/remarriage situations
- Blended family groups
- Retirement
- Re-filled nest when the children return home with their children
- When children leave the nest to go out on their own
- Home health care
- Managing dual career marriages

Sketch your plan to become intentional about "as you go" throughout your work week, times of play and leisure, and personal crises. Who are the people seeking God and what are the entry points for you to network with them? What are the issues they are working with? What type of learners are they? What is the best time to meet with them?

As an example, let's say you have several persons in your church and or community who are dealing with aging parents. Of course we want discipleship plan to come out of not only the shared burden and calling or passion of the people, but the needs and gifts of leaders too.

Those who have gone before down this life passage and have learned from it and grown through it can facilitate this part of the church's ministry. This particular discipleship team might design something that looks like the following:

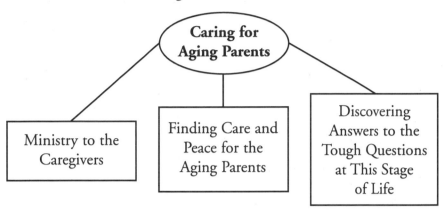

Notice the spiritual formation is really at three different points of need, three different levels of risks and issues of vulnerability. Those in the community, who are not a consistent part of the community of faith, could enter at the "ministry to caregiver" or "finding care for the aging parent" phase with some degree of ease and practicality. Those seeking spiritual answers and searching for meaning might move to the third more disciplined subject. It seems that building experiences around such life needs/issues would create appropriate and relevant forums for discipleship designed to meet people where they are, grow them forward in faith and life, and provide connection with persons on a similar journey as part of the community of faith. As a comfortable nonthreatening entry point, you might publicize this in the city/community newspaper, nursing home bulletin boards, doctor's offices, pharmacies, through those in the church related to medical community or home health care system. Do a weekend seminar in a hotel banquet hall or community center. Be sure to bring in a capable leader for the event. Have in place the support and follow up small group system (described above) to offer to all those who participate.

From a traditional Sunday school class perspective, I've found that a person who can be the "discipleship point person" helps insure that no one's spiritual journey is ignored, taken for granted, or goes unprepared for. Discuss this with your class as a strategy for outgrowing those believers who have become ingrown in their attitudes, relationships and ministries.

Reframing Hints To Ponder

- There are many spiritually thirsty people in the world but few of them are going to church.
- A prevalent reality of our age is the ingrown nature of many churches.
- The purpose of the church is not pastoral care of the membership, but the evangelization of the world.
- There are many ways of evaluating how ingrown your church is.
- Outgrowing an ingrown church takes a clear vision of the biblical purpose of the church, a commitment to focusing on that mission, good planning skills, conflict management skills, patience, prayer, and intentionality.
- Very often an ingrown church is not being led by the Holy Spirit but by the personal preferences of a small group of leaders living in their comfort zones.
- Part of the challenge for an ingrown church is to shift values from "taking care of us" to "taking care of us and reaching them."

When a Church Doesn't Want to Be Led

As I travel across our state and other parts of the country working with pastors, staff, and church leaders I hear frequently, "I'm in a church that doesn't want to be led." Other words of grief, frustration and a wringing of hands wondering where to go from here usually accompany this comment.

As I seek to clarify exactly what is meant by the statement I discover that the leader talking with me perceives that:

- Certain people (matriarchs or patriarchs) have made it clear they have been and will always be the leaders in given congregations.
- Certain committees (usually deacons, personnel, and/or finance committees) have their own ideas about the way things should be done (usually the way we've always done it) and aren't interested in new ideas or practices.

- Certain organizations (usually WMU, choir, or a given Sunday School class) have their own ideas about the way they have done things and their passion to see that it continues.
- Tradition is the leader that prevents the trying of new ideas or strategies.
- The pastor is blocked in leading the church because someone or something keeps getting in the way.

Possibilities for Moving Forward When the Pressure is On

The very essence of leadership is taking up the mantel and moving forward when others aren't up to or interested in the task. Granted, controlling members, committees, or families can be difficult to deal with and often create a threatening atmosphere for the leader. I've run into this in every church I've served in. Mr. B, a charter member, had invested himself and his money in a church and felt this earned him the right to control decisions of the church. He controlled every business meeting. Then there was the long time church member who was the financial secretary — she controlled the information flow, the money flow, the calendar and the budget. The list could go on.

What I learned through these situations and many others is that more often than not these blocks to the church's progress had more to do with my skills as a leader than their stubbornness as members. Now let me be quick to say, life and ministry would have been much more fulfilling, enjoyable, and exciting if these controllers were not so controlling and hard-headed. I do believe that the controllers need to rethink their commitment. Are they more committed to the community of faith and the biblical mandates for the church or are they more committed to their personal preferences, comfort zones, or traditions? This is a critical question and spiritual issue for them and all of us to ponder regularly. It is so easy to fall into the trap of personal preferences and lose sight of God's preferences and commands. Let's be careful.

Certainly leadership is an issue not to be ignored. Let's explore some possibilities of moving forward when such pressure is on:

- Use the opportunity to do a spiritual life and leadership skill inventory. Are there issues to be resolved within you or with the other parties involved? If so, get with it!
- Pray, pray, and get others you trust to pray about the situation and people involved.
- Confront the situation head on — don't dance around it or ignore it. Believe me, it will not go away without working with it/them at some level.
- Cultivate the relationship, even though you may not want to, with the controlling person/group involved. Meet them on their turf. Get to know their dreams, visions, desires, and heartaches and share your own as God leads.
- Remember, when making change of any kind in the life of an organization — *change values before you change structures.*
- If this relational avenue doesn't bear some fruit within six months, then talk with other key leaders and pray about whether to work around the controllers and create a parallel structure to basically leave them/their group alone.
- Seek to enlist people with new vision, openness, and yearning into new organizations and be ready to serve as a midwife to birth the new. Understand that birthing is often painful and involves a period of spiritual pregnancy and gestation. Be patient, nurture those giving birth to the new and pray.

Bill Easum has written about the birthing of the new and the ministry of being a midwife in his *Growing Spiritual Redwoods*. I've dealt with these struggles and value shifts in *Making the Church Work*.

Finding the Strength to Go On

If you've honestly tried, prayed, done a spiritual life and leadership assessment, worked at cultivating relationships, and it's still not working, explore other options. Maybe it's time to start a parallel track to meet the ministry need.

Far too often we tend to let the controllers give us ulcers, create paralyzing fear in our lives and ministry, and distract us from our calling and God's leadership. Rather than letting the controllers do this to you, maybe it's time to work on your leadership skills, conflict management skills, build a support group network and accountability group of others to help you keep perspective, and keep moving forward in your life and ministry. Running from every tough situation doesn't help us or the church mature.

Reframing Hints To Ponder

- The very essence of leadership is taking up the mantel and moving forward when others aren't up to it or interested in the task.
- It's very easy to fall into the trap of personal preferences and lose sight of God's preferences and commands.
- Far too often we tend to let the controllers give us ulcers, create paralyzing fear in our lives and ministry and distract us from our calling and God's leadership.

Who Is Leading Your Church?

Leadership is key in most institutions these days. Who is leading your church? Some would immediately say the pastor and/or staff. Others would say the deacons. Still others might say the church council, trustees, or a patriarch or matriarch. Let me suggest that we look at this question from a different perspective. Is your church being lead by traditions of the past, dominant personalities, comfort zones, or God's calling?

When the Past Is Leading

When the traditions and successes of the past are leading a church many conversations and meetings frequently seem to...

- Be filled with phrases like, "when so and so was here or when we did such and such things were better"; or "do you remember when"; or "If we'd just do things like we did in 10 years ago things would be better."
- Focus on the past rather than dreams for the future.
- Be overly concerned with survival and maintenance issues rather than mission challenges and opportunities.

As we move into the next century, church leaders are being challenged and called to move from the past into the future. This is not to say that the past leaders or successes were not of value — indeed they were. However the realities of our world have drastically changed and the church is being called to change too. Throughout church history our *forms* have changed with the times so that the message of the Gospel can be clearly understood and the *function* of the church be accomplished. The New Testament is clear: the forms of the church are much less important than the function of the church. Unfortunately today most churches are wrestling with forms and ignoring the function and thus minimizing the Great Commission.

Have you encountered any of these characteristics in your church? Or in yourself?

When Dominant Personalities Are Leading

Another leader in many of our churches are those dominant personalities from the past or present. It may be long-term pastors or staff members who have long since retired or died. It may be a long-term deacon chair, charter family, a long term secretary or strong personality involved in leadership for many years (a matriarch or patriarch). Such leaders certainly have their place in the church history, however when the future of the church is being controlled or dominated by persons with an agenda or persons who have long since left the church, the church's future is likely in danger. God has gifted the body of Christ with various gifts and each part of the membership has a vital voice and function in the Body of Christ. When dominant personalities are leading you often see . . .

- Power struggles between the dominant personality and persons who want to move beyond that person's leadership.
- Have a large silent majority who choose for various reasons not to challenge the dominant personality out of respect, fear or anger.
- A growing apathy in other leaders who have learned over time not "to rock the boat" or "go against the dominant person."
- Financial concerns or controls used as a threat against the congregation or pastoral leadership.

Have you seen or experienced any of these characteristics in your church?

When Comfort Zones Are Leading

One of the greatest threats to the future of the church is the reality that many churches and many church leaders like living in the comfort zones of leadership rather than leading toward effectiveness and out of faithfulness. When comfort zones are leading you often see . . .

- Leaders who shift calendar events from one year to the next without much thought, planning, or evaluation.
- Congregations who resist change at most every level. They like who they are and don't plan to change.
- Pastors/staff who are living in frustration for they see the need to change and yet they are living among persons whose favorite song is "We shall not be moved."
- Congregations who are content to take care of their own, not reach out to others and who have a "survival or maintenance" mentality.
- Leaders who walk by sight and not by faith.

We must remember the lives of the children of Israel, Abraham and Sarah, Paul, Stephen, Priscilla and Aquila, and Peter, who taught us that the call of God is to move us beyond our comfort zones. Our hunger for comfort, security and self-preservation is choking the life out of the church of today and is certain to sabotage the churches effectiveness in the twenty-first century.

When the Leader Is God's Call

The effective congregation in the twenty-first century is certain to follow the mandates God laid before us long ago. The bold brave lives and risk-taking ministries of those founders of the faith (Heb 11) and the courage and innovative spirits of the founders of the early church (Acts) are still our role models. When God called Moses to lead God's people from bondage, no excuse was sufficient. Moses chose to follow God and moved beyond many of his personal comfort zones in order to be obedient to God's call. And then there were Peter, Paul, Stephen, and countless other leaders of the early church. They moved beyond comfort to care for the Samaritans and the Gentiles. The risk the early church fathers took was simply astounding. The culture and challenge they encountered are no different from the challenge and culture we are faced with.

When God's call is the leader, you frequently encounter...

- Persons of intense prayer who desire to please God.
- Persons who are on a spiritual journey and are seeking God.
- Congregations who are living by faith and not by sight.
- Congregations who don't concern themselves with meeting the line of their budget, but in being faithful to God's call.
- Risk-taking leaders who want to penetrate the culture with the message of Christ.

Have you encountered these issues/people in your congregation? Who is leading your church? Who is your leader?

Reframing Hints To Ponder

- Is your church being led by traditions of the past, dominate personalities, comfort zones or God's calling?
- Church leaders are being called to move from the past into the future.
- Biblical personalities teach us that the call of God is to move us beyond our comfort zones.
- Our hunger for comfort, security and self-preservation is choking the life out of the church today and stabotaging the effectiveness of the church in the twenty-first century.

Managing Change: Guiding Shifts to Ensure Effective Ministry

Many of the principles in this book will lead most leaders and congregations to engage with change and transition at one or more levels. In most incidences church leaders have not received training in how to manage change or transition. The following is an attempt to highlight some basic principles and resources that might help leaders in facilitating changes they sense God leading them to make in their respective congregations or lives.

Creating a Dual Track Ministry: Managing the Present While Birthing the Future

Over the years I've watched many churches and leaders try to implement change and I've been a part of many transitional organizations and teams myself. I've seen change handled effectively and I've seen it become the hub of chaos and pain.

Let me review some of the principles that I've found to be most helpful as churches seek to manage the present (for the church culture) while at the same time birth the future church (to reach those from the unchurched culture):

- Change values *before* you change structures. This is so important. It takes time, effort and intentionality to work with core leaders and legitmizers to help them shift from a "caring for us mentality" to "reaching them mentality and conviction."
- When seeking to implement structural changes, don't neglect emotional and relational dimensions of transitioning. Change brings emotional and often relational discomfort. That doesn't mean the change is bad or "out of God's will" — it simply means that change touches our hearts, our comfort zones, and our routine relationships.
- Seek to involve leadership and followers in the revisioning process. Seek to build ownership among a broad base of leaders and followers to help fashion the new.
- Seek to discern God's timing and follow God's leading rather than the personal preferences of a leader or a small group's agenda. Praying always that God might lead and "go before" and prepare the way for the changes and transitions God desires.
- Be intentional about identifying and working with the remnant — those who hear a new voice for a new vision or those who are willing to count the cost of birthing the new. The principle of the remnant has strong roots in the ministry of Jesus and in the

management concepts of bringing about change. You start with the adopters, continue with the adapters, and don't wait on the mass or the laggards to begin. Start small and then work the systems of influence each person has and create a new working model for all to see and experience.

• Validate the ministries that speak to those in existing effective ministries — those that are primarily designed for the church culture. While at the same time be intentional about birthing the new ministries that reach the unchurched and nurture those with a spiritual thirst by meeting them where they are. This might include alternative worship services, Bible Study group, life issue groups, personal issue groups or recreational and leisure entry points. Frequently it is this challenge that creates most of the intensity and confusion.7

Much of the change and transition we face as leaders and churches begins when we change the way we think. The change of the way we think creates change in the way we behave or respond to questions of the post modern person without becoming defensive or preachy. Rick Richardson offers excellent help in this venue with his book *Evangelism Outside the Box*.5 Here are the eight questions he poses to challenge us to rethink and reframe our evangelistic efforts in a postmodern world:

(1) **Questions of power and motive**. Even our logical answers can feel like an exercise of colonizing power. To many people we're just another tribe, using logic to gain power. Postmodern people have redefined truth as "whatever rings true to your experience, whatever feels real to you." There's no grand story to inspire people. Any attempt to claim that one has the truth for everybody is heard as an arrogant attempt at domination and control.

(2) **Questions of identity**. Who am I? Who will I listen to for help in developing my identity and sense of self? How can you Christians think you can tell other people who they are? Who do you think you are to invalidate my sense of self and identity and my group's definition of who we are?

(3) **Questions of pain and suffering**. Why do I hurt? Why did my family break apart? Why is there so much hatred and violence in the world? People are crying out not so much for philosophical answers as for a way to give meaning and purpose to personal and corporate suffering.

(4) **Questions of character, trust and attractiveness**. Why should I trust you? Look at what believers have done: racism, sexism, homophobia, the Crusades, religious wars. Intolerance and narrow hate seem to mark your institutions. Your character is no better than the character of the society you live in. I can trust you just as much as I can trust other leaders in our society — which is hardly at all.

(5) **Questions of love and meaning**. How can you reject the homosexual lifestyle? How can you say you love people when you reject who they are, how they define their very identity? How can you question living together when people love each other? How can you be rule-oriented in your ethics when the situation has to determine what is really loving?

(6) **Questions of interpretation**. Isn't the way you see the world completely dependent on your community and place of birth? Can't you interpret Scripture any way you want, and haven't you? I don't care about the Bible's reliability. I am concerned about its integrity and moral value. After all, it was written by patriarchal, ethnocentric people.

(7) **Questions of relevance and relativism**. Does your belief change lives? Does prayer really make a difference? Does your religion help you with your pain? If it works for you, why should it work for me? What does it matter what you believe as long as it works and helps you? The question of the uniqueness of Christ is not primarily philosophical as it is utilitarian. Don't all religions help people equally? If a religion works and feels real to a person, then it is true for that person. People are not looking for theological comparisons but for attractiveness and relevance.

(8) **Questions of impact.** Does your religion help society? Does it help me, whether I'm in your group or not? Or are you just another self-serving group?

Reframing Hints To Ponder

- Managing change is a challenge for churches that most church leaders are not prepared to manage.
- Creating a Dual Track Ministry is an avenue for managing the present while birthing the future.
- A major change to be worked with concerns our evangelistic model and strategy as we seek to minister in an unchurched culture.

Building Accountability — Creating Opportunities for Moving People Forward in Faith

Helping people move forward in their faith is a challenge churches and leaders face. Church people need the focus, motivation, and evidence of fruitfulness of their participation in church. The unchurched who are spiritually thirsty need the roadmap for pursuing meaning in life and networking with resources and fellow strugglers to help nurture them in their journey. George Barna's research indicates that there is little difference in the demographics of the churched and unchurched. He further explains that 42 percent of the unchurched have a nominal Christian commitment. In a typical week five out of ten of them pray to God, three out of ten have a devotional time, one out of seven reads from the Bible.[6]

Many churches and believers claim they are serious about discipleship, however very few, only one out of five according to George Barna, are serious about facilitating discipleship and only one out of five believers have measurable and specific goals for personal spiritual growth.[7] It has been my personal observation and experience over the last decade that many churched and unchurched persons have a craving and deep desire for a roadmap to health, wholeness, and spiritual growth. They attend churches but find little talk about discipleship, in most cases. Most churches and believers do not want to put in the work of prayer, planning, and customizing to chart a course of spiritual formation for families, individuals, classes, and groups. Many are afraid of evaluating spiritual growth. After all, many say, "spiritual growth is such a personal thing." The thirst for maturity and ridding oneself of hindrances and baggage from the past is a challenge many face. There's a need for tracks to walk persons out of "the wilderness" into a "land of milk and honey."

Charting a Course Through the Wilderness

In order to build in accountability and discipline into the body of Christ, a roadmap is essential. Unless people know what they are aiming for they will never know if the goal has been met. What are the landmarks in the journey out of the wilderness and into the land of milk and honey? What are the pathways? It seems to me that the ministry of Christ with the twelve had several landmarks or indicators in their journey toward maturity.

• Spending time with Christ
• Learning to love Him and walk with Him
• Developing Christian virtues and fruits of the Spirit
• Developing patience
• Reaching out to others
• Ministering the poor and needy

So how might individuals and groups evaluate these and other indicators? Once these measuring devices are in place, then accountability can be generated as a pathway toward wholeness and health. Small groups, one on one relationships, mentoring relationships, accountability relationships in family systems, and small groups provide opportunities to help others lovingly move forward in faith. Establishing covenantal relationships around attainable spiritual life goals provides motivation to move forward, goals to strive for, virtues, and characteristics to work on within the context of the body of Christ and healthy relationships. Attaining goals and celebrating steps in maturity is a motivator to keep moving forward.

What then facilitates accountability in the church? Corporate accountability doesn't emerge until personal/individual accountability is modeled and proven effective in spiritual formation. Here are some hints that I've found helpful in facilitating:

Personal Accountability:

- Establish personal and spiritual growth goals. Share with a support person or group for purposes of accountability. (Spiritual Life Inventories are helpful in goal setting/evaluation.)
- Form accountability groups/relationships around those areas that you are working in. This will serve as a check/balance for your growth.
- Invite someone into your world as an accountability person. Set specific times/places where you will report on the progress made in assigned, mutually agreed upon growth areas.
- Be certain to design, with your accountability group/partner, a specific reading list, prayer list, and "to do list" that will facilitate growth.
- Discuss with your accountability person(s) the consequences of not fulfilling your accountability covenant (personal, spiritual, relational, family, financial).
- Covenant with the accountability person/group honesty, sensitivity, intercessory prayer and continuity of dialogue.

Corporate Accountability:

- Clarity and ownership of vision of lay ministry will provide seeds of accountability for members to hold each other accountable to stated philosophy, objectives and goals
- Reinforcement of vision of ministry provided through relevant sermons, curricula designs and ministry opportunities. (*The Doctrine of the Laity* by Findley B. Edge is very helpful with this.)
- Corporate reporting of ministries within the body where members can share what God is doing in and through them as representatives of the church in the world.

- Provide a place and time for "sounding the call" when the church gathers so that others might serve as role models and enlist others in ministry.
- Set and publish specific goals that will move the church to be the kind of church that will facilitate lay ministry.
- Follow-up on goals through dialogue sessions, commitment times and challenge.
- Create opportunities for persons to invite others into their lives as accountability partners.

Helping the churched and those who are spiritually thirsty but are unchurched find and follow the landmarks, road signs and pathways to a fuller more meaningful life and faith are challenges we must take seriously. What are the landmarks you are moving toward in your Christian walk as they apply to:

- Parenting
- Marriage
- Work life
- Temperament
- Crises
- Investing your time and resources
- Your circle of friends and relationships
- Your biblical knowledge
- Your involvement in leadership and service

These are simply illustrative of arenas one might explore as pathways to moving forward in faith. What's your next step?

Reframing Hints To Ponder

- Accountability is essential in building a disciplined body and a forward moving faith formation.
- There's little difference in the demographics of the churched and unchurched.
- Many believers and churches claim they are serious about discipleship, but most have no strategic and accountable plan.
- Discovering and implementing a measuring instrument for one's spiritual formation and progress is essential in the culture in which we minister today.

Reinventing Ministry in a Secular Culture

Ministering in the twenty-first century is filled with many complexities. The beginning of this new decade has brought deep pain, remorse, grief, hopelessness, anxiety, confusion, and aimlessness for many ministers. The turbulent and rapid changes in our society and culture are complicated by the schisms in our own denominations. Such complexities and challenges are now causing professional crises, family strife and personal struggles with integrity, self-esteem, and fulfillment of calling for many ministers. There is a crying need to help today's minister, who finds themselves in these crises, to reinvent and reframe ministry. I am one of those ministers. Let me share some of the issues I'm working with, and beginning to help others work with, in order to rediscover personal and professional fulfillment in the twenty-first century.

The Crises in Review

Ever since my seminary days, my Southern Baptist denomination has been in a state of tension, controversy, and crisis. Some say its been a struggle for control; others say it's over theological differences; others suggest it's a shift in culture and generations. Whatever the reason, during my service in and through local churches, seminary classrooms, and numerous associational and denominational committees, I've noted that these crises have moved from a debate behind closed doors at a national level to strategies that are now impacting local churches, associations, and state conventions. Beyond that, the crisis is manifesting itself in the lives and families of our ministers. I have numerous friends who have already left the denomination or have shifted to secular vocations in order to try to reclaim balance, integrity, fulfillment, or focus.

Now I'm encountering colleagues on a regular basis who feel "trapped" in ministry. Their education, networking options, and calling places them within the denominational circles of ministry and yet they are finding fewer and fewer places for fulfillment of their calling. Many feel disengaged, isolated, or alienated from the denomination they grew up in. Others feel they want to get out of the ministry, because of the pressures on their family and the trivialities local churches demand they attend to daily. But their network, training, and options are restricted. Ministers are "burning out" daily; many are divorcing; others are losing their children to outside forces; many are on anti-depressants and most are working far too many hours in order to "please the powers that be" in their churches. They feel guilty because they are "appeasing the power groups" in their churches and neglecting the biblical mandate and their personal calling. Many of our churches somehow believe that their ministers are present to "take care of them" rather than "equip them to do the work of ministry" (Eph 4). The pressure is intense. How does one seek to be faithful to one's calling and the biblical mandate for the church when your members want you to be at their beckoned call for "pastoral care"? The pastoral care model of the mid- to late-1900s seems to be more important to most of our churches than the disciplemaking pastor model of the 2000s.

If clergy and lay leaders are going to experience a renewal of heart and meaningfulness for ministry some serious efforts at reinventing and reframing of ministry is called for. Reframing ministry calls forth a reinventing of ministry for those inside professional roles and for those sitting in the pews of our churches.

The secular condition of our world is pushing the clergy into equipping roles rather than management, preaching or pastoral care roles. The demands our churches have made on clergy amidst a growing and deepening pastoral care need is a source of the burnout that many feel. Ministry was never intended by God to be in the hands of a few, but in the hands of *all* believers. Somehow and somewhere this Biblical cornerstone of Christianity was turned into a ministry dominated and often controlled by clergy and relinquished by lay persons.

The secular world is applying pressure to the believer in the pew who has been more of a passive spectator than an active participant in ministry. For if the secular world is to find and experience the message of Christ the believer must take it into the world — a few ordained clergy can't do it all alone. If this mission is approached then the clergy must equip and the institutional church must become more than a place for believers. The local church must become a hospital for the broken and hurting and a site for evangelism as they learn to be the salt, light and leaven into the world.

A reinventing of the way we define our effectiveness and success as staff or believers who are members of a congregation confronts us. A reinventing of curricula models and leadership models is also coming under scrutiny and challenge.

Lessons from the Engel Scale

For reinventing to happen a reframing must occur. A new cognitive map must be created, new standards, new tools and resources and strategies. The Engel Scale has been worked with by many for over a decade. Each number in the scale notes a step in the spiritual journey of those living in and moving from a secular and unchurched culture into the life and work of the church.

Engel Scale of Spiritual Decision

+5 Stewardship
+4 Communion with God
+3 Conceptual and behavioral growth
+2 Incorporation into Body
+1 Post-decision evaluation
New birth
-1 Repentance and faith in Christ
-2 Decision to act
-3 Personal problem recognition
-4 Positive attitude towards Gospel
-5 Grasp implications of Gospel
-6 Awareness of fundamentals of Gospel
-7 Initial awareness of Gospel
-8 Awareness of supreme being, no knowledge of Gospel

Don't be put off because it looks mathematical! For instance, when someone has come to realize they have a spiritual problem, they are at -3 on the scale. If we understand roughly where a person (or a whole target group of people) stand spiritually on this scale, we can adjust the way that we present the Gospel to them.

Others have suggested different refinements of the Engel Scale. Frank Gray of FEBC Radio has proposed a horizontal axis of antagonism/enthusiasm. It is a remarkably simple but enlightening concept because it helps us to visualize important evangelistic concepts. Christian evangelistic communication has often failed to touch people who are low down the scale, because it has been presented in Christian language and thought-forms and has not engaged with those it was intended for. The tragedy is that so often, evangelism is only touching the "once-churched" (those with some Christian background) rather than the "never-churched" (those who know nothing of the Gospel at all). The lower-left oval shape represents a person or group of people who are fairly resistant and lack knowledge. The challenge to us is always to use approaches that reach down as far as possible into the bottom left-hand corner![8]

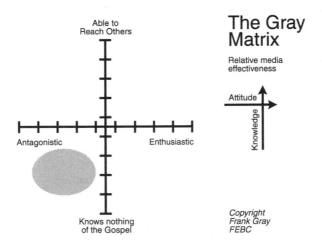

Effective evangelism not only requires people to obtain more knowledge they must also move from a position of antagonism/indifference to a more positive viewpoint. They are unlikely to wish to find out more until they view Christianity more positively.

• Anything which moves people from left to right across the scale is "evangelistic." This might include acts of service and friendship, mum and baby clubs, medical and development work - many things which are not apparently "preaching." Yet in fact, the word Jesus used when he told us to "preach the Gospel" has a much wider meaning than speech it refers to communication. (There is a Christian debt-counseling service in UK, where 80 percent of those helped are eventually converted!) For some people groups, apologies offered for the past historical actions of groups perceived to be "Christian" are also healing hurts and reducing antagonism to the Gospel.

• If we can understand roughly where a single person or target group of people is situated on the scale, we can choose an appropriate approach to reach them.

• If people are near the bottom of the scale, we must not use Christian language and ideas that will mean nothing to them. We must assess our message through their eyes, not ours. It may also be inappropriate to give a heavy "preach for a decision" at this point.

• Pressures of society and culture, and the strategies of the Enemy will tend to pull people down towards the bottom left-hand of the scale. God's purpose is to draw people to the top right-hand side by his Spirit, through the witness of his people.

Communication Challenges for Discipleship in a Secular Culture

Another adaptation of the Engel Scale comes from the work of Bill Bright and Mark McCloskey.9 As they view it, communication is a learned art. It is easier for some of us than for others. Some of us are naturally outgoing and can tune in to other's feelings more easily. Some of us are withdrawn and fearful of making contact with others, even on a superficial level. But regardless of our personality type and gifts (or lack of them) in the area of communication, most of start out on the bottom rung of the ladder as "self-centered" communicators.

THE ROAD TO OTHER-CENTERED COMMUNICATION

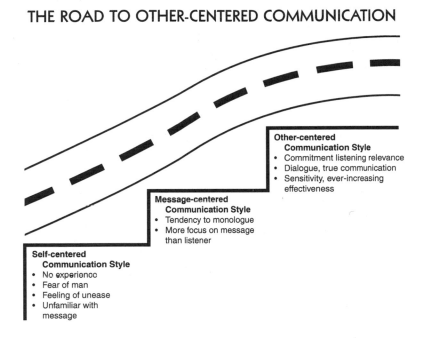

Other-centered Communication Style
- Commitment listening relevance
- Dialogue, true communication
- Sensitivity, ever-increasing effectiveness

Message-centered Communication Style
- Tendency to monologue
- More focus on message than listener

Self-centered Communication Style
- No experience
- Fear of man
- Feeling of unease
- Unfamiliar with message

The Self-Centered Communicator

A self-centered communicator is one whose attention is focused on oneself. Most of us find it difficult, if not impossible, just to be ourselves and act naturally when another person is present and we sense that he may be evaluating us. What happened the last time you were told, "Just act naturally. I want to take your picture"? Did your attention automatically turn inward as you asked yourself, *How is my hair? Is my best side showing?* Did you become self-conscious to the point of discomfort?

We find ourselves dealing with the same tendencies in our first attempts to witness to others about Christ. The fear of being rejected, the lack of experience, and the discomfort that comes from doing something new all force us to turn our attention inward and ask, What does this person think of me? Does he think I'm strange, talking about Jesus like this? Lord, help me get through this conversation. I hope my mouthwash is still working. The result of this inward focus is communication with limited effectiveness. With all our energy and attention focused on these questions, there is little left for dealing with the concerns of message fidelity and feedback.

The Message-Oriented Communicator

The message-oriented communicator asks himself, "Am I doing justice to the content and intent of the message?" "How am I doing in terms of fidelity?" But as the figure shows, this phase stills falls short of true other-centered communication. The communicator's energies are focused on the message, not on the listener.

What is the best way to free yourself to invest your emotional energies in the listener? The answer is to master the message to such a degree that it becomes second nature to you. Only then can your communication energies be focused on the listener. This is why concentrating on a particular format for sharing the gospel is so important, for the sooner I master the message, the sooner I can move into the most efficient realm of communication, the other-centered style.

The Other-Centered Communicator

The other-centered communication style does not happen by accident. It is the result of hard work, experience and training. In a real sense it is a privilege, reserved for those who have mastered their message and overcome the fears and inertia that would otherwise rob them of life-giving conversations about Christ with their friends, neighbors and anyone else who will listen.

Such research offers additional clues for reinventing ministry for the twenty-first century. Where would you assess yourself in light of this chart? What would make you more effective in communicating effectively the Good News?

Reframing Ministry Refreshes Meaning

The reframing of ministry for our age can refresh the minister and the biblical mission so that personal and professional fulfillment can be experienced and the church can become pleasing to God. Let me suggest some reframing to consider personally and corporately as the body of Christ as you search for greater effectiveness in the twenty-first century.

• **Reframe "minister" and "ministry."** Review the biblical nature of minister and ministry. A review and realignment of our language and practices is called for during these days of change and stress. Let's revisit a serious biblical study of the nature and mission of the people of God. You will likely discover that *all* God's people are "ministers" and *all* believers are responsible for "ministry" in the church and in the world. God has given all believers gifts and calls all believers to be "sent" and to "be on mission." The implications of this alone would revolutionize most churches if we took it seriously. The essence of this doctrine has been talked about for decades, now we are being challenged by the conditions of our day and church to reclaim, redeem, and flesh out these incarnational concepts in our world.

• **Reframe "church."** Exploring the biblical nature of "church" is simply an extension of the first issue I suggest you explore. The scripture is clear about the mission of the people of God. The Great Commission calls us to "go into all the world," to "be scattered as salt, light and leaven in the world." We are the "bride of Christ" in a relationship with God. The church "gathered" is a time of celebration and equipping for ministry of ALL the people of God and a time of connecting with God for instructions for the week. Christianity is a seven day a week faith, not one day of week "churchianity." (My book, *The Gathered and Scattered Church*, might also help you with this reframing.)

Such reframing of church gives challenge and freedom for many. For ministry and church can be, must be done, not just inside the church walls, during the gathered times during the week, but ministry and church is done also *in the* world. Maybe all those who are "leaving the ministry" in the institutional church, are actually revitalizing the "scattered church" in the world. What a wonderful and much needed thing in an unchurched culture! How can we affirm and equip this scattered church? An encouraging illustration of this is the proliferation of "FBOs" (faith based organizations) that are emerging all across our country. The corporate world is calling pastors to shepherd their workforce, many of which find more spiritual direction and community there than in the institutional churches of which they are a part they pass every day.

• **Reframe Christian Education**. Since the 1950s Christian education in most Baptist churches has been defined by programs — Sunday School, Discipleship Training, Worship, WMU, Baptist Men. We met at assigned times, in assigned places, read from literature prepared at a national level and was denominationally driven and prepared for a specific group of persons. In those days we were living in a "church culture" where we had enjoyed "a million more in '54" and most persons in our communities had fairly favorable feelings toward "religious language and experiences." Now that is no longer true. Pluralism of cultures, traditions and people groups have emerged. Now almost 70 percent of our population is considered "unchurched."

The time is here to reframe Christian education. A more relational model, a life-based, need oriented model is emerging. It's not bound by space, time, and literature. It can be done over the internet, via teleconferencing, through coaching and mentoring relationships, in house gatherings, in the business office, during a lunch break or family vacation and yes still in groups and classes that meet at assigned times inside the walls of the church building.

Again, maybe, through all the stress and shifting of "ministers," God is raising up another needed dimension and workforce for a decentralized model of Christian education. Could it be that God is retooling, through our pain and struggle, a new generation, new breed of church leader, minister and even church structure for building God's kingdom? Could it be that we have been so focused on building our budgets, staffs, buildings and denominations that we have neglected the building of God's Kingdom and penetrating His world as the salt, light and leaven amidst the forces of the world? Could it be that we are moving back to the style of ministry of the first generation church found in the book of Acts?

Reframing Hints To Ponder

- Reframing is needed for replenishing the meaning of professional ministry.
- Reinventing is called for if the clergy and lay persons are to be effective in this secular culture
- Finding and following more effective communication styles will be increasingly important to insure an effective ministry in our secular and unchurched culture.

Reinventing Staff for Today's and Tomorrow's Churches

More often than not church leadership takes on the priorities and personality of those guiding their spiritual formation. If the clergy are maintaining programs and only sustaining an institution you can expect the leaders and congregation to move in that direction. In a secular and paganistic world it is vital that the spiritual leadership have at their heart making and reproducing healthy disciples.

As the world around our churches and the population inside our churches change there's increasing pressure to reinvent staff to insure effectiveness in discipleship, outreach and inreach ministries. Dual career marriages, diversity of family structures and people groups, shifting demographics, early retirements, economic shifts, home-based businesses and the impact of technology on daily life seem to be creating an atmosphere that calls forth new directions in staffing churches. While some churches are already experimenting with new configurations, new ministry descriptions, titles and compensation packages many others continue to work from titles, descriptions, and packages from the 1950s and 1960s and are fueling the burnout rate among ministers today.

Burnout's Connections to Outdated Staffing

Over the past 10 years I've noted an increasing number of excellent, committed, and called clergy who are struggling with or have been consumed by burnout. Some of the connections I've noted between the threats of burnout and out of date staffing issues are: Many clergy . . .

- Are overworked because the needs and demands in their parish are intensifying and multiplying because of the rapid changes around them.
- Suffer because of a lack of continuing education. While the pace of life is rapid, many churches do not encourage or support ongoing education so the clergy can stay current.
- Families are faced with personal struggles like all other families and yet many clergy are not given permission or encouragement to take care of their families. They are almost affirmed for sacrificing their family's health so they can take care of others.
- Struggle with their physical health because the demands and expectations of most congregations are so great. Again they are expected to sacrifice their health to "take care of others' needs."
- Are underpaid when compared to other professionals, with similar education and experience, in their communities. Therefore financial pressures are intense. Sometimes second jobs are required to financial stability and this creates more stress in family and congregation.
- Have a growing dissatisfaction with their ministries and their ability to find fulfillment and effectiveness in ministry.
- Are locked into "job descriptions" designed to maintain the institution rather than freed by "ministry descriptions" designed to empower them to work from their calling and gifting.

Other Indicators of Ineffectiveness of Current Staffing

While burnout is one indicator of the need to rethink and reframe staffing, there are other issues that point to the increasing ineffectiveness of our current models of staffing our churches:

- Increasing number of mismatches between clergy and congregations that creates tensions for both parties.
- Most churches and most church leaders (including clergy) continue to function from values, mindsets and traditions from a modern world, a church culture — when the reality is we are now in a

postmodern, unchurched culture. Consequently most of our energies and priorities reflect a modern culture and the unchurched have no advocate in our midst and the post-modern world is not addressed.

- The definitions of our success/effectiveness for our staff and churches are still based on modern and churched culture standards. Such only creates more tensions and ineffectiveness.
- Dysfunction seems to have deep roots in many of our existing congregations, leadership cores and clergy. Such has created a real sense of control and dysfunctional, neurotic organizations we call churches. Until we have healthy leaders we are not likely to have healthy churches.
- Some of the best clergy, pulpiteers and pastors I know are leaving the professional ministry and entering vocations in the business world. Their bottom line reason is "I just can't fight this system any longer — my people want to play power games, they don't want to do and be church!"
- We've lost balance in ministry. Focusing too much on institutional maintenance and survival rather than perpetuation of mission and ministry to the hurting, lost, spiritually thirsty and broken of our world.

Models to Consider When Reinventing Staff

Current models of staffing churches seem to be focused more on institutional maintenance and caring for the flock than activating the people of God on mission. We have pastors who are "hired to lead in worship, marry the engaged, bury the dead, to visit the sick and lonely, administrate the variety of church based meetings, and raise the money for institutional programming" — rather than pastors who are called to equip the laity to do the work of ministry. We expect and hire our pastors to do the work of ministry.

Many of our churches cling to this care-giving model while the Ephesians 4 model of staffing is that of an "equipper of the saints for the work of ministry." Seems this biblical model of equipping of the saints (the people in the pew — the believers and members of the congregation) has given way to pastoral care, pastor driven model to "take care of us at all costs" and "perform for us upon demand." Such a model that we've embraced and practiced for decades has created a vast number of spectator congregations, a host of God's frozen chosen and generated not an active army of the people of God on mission, but an apathetic self-absorbed congregation that has lost sight of the biblical mandate of "going into all the world" with the mission of God, as God's missionaries.

Now we do have other staff positions — Ministers of education, youth, children, families, senior adults, administration, etc. Some poor souls even have *all* of these people groups in their title! However in most situations the job descriptions again revolve more around "taking care of us and performing for us" rather than "equipping us to reach and disciple them." How did we ever get into such a narcissistic place with our staffing? What would have happened if Jesus had come to earth just to "take care of the twelve or the inner circle of three"? He did spend much time with this remnant, but for the purpose of equipping them to carry his message into all the world. Such a focus insured that his mission reach us. If he had only been on a pastoral care mission our generation would have never known His message.

I'm certain that some of you are now either feeling defensive or ecstatic. Some readers will say the church minister should "take care of us" and others will say "it's about time someone pointed out the churches narcissism tendencies in its staff!" If you're not too upset let's explore some of the emerging models of staffing that are built upon equipping, discipling rather than just institutional maintenance.

Emerging models of staffing churches is a struggle only the brave, courageous and faithful face today for staffing issues touches personal comfort zones, institutional and personal identities and self image as well as one's theological assumptions about church and ministers. So as we outline some emerging models keep in mind these struggles in yourself and among your leadership and congregation. Remember too, that more often than not the congregation takes on the personality and focus of its lay and clergy leadership. Here are some examples of followed leadership focus:

• **Mission/Ministry Focus** – When mission and ministry become the focus of the professional staff the typical congregation faces the realities that their staff no longer exist to "serve them" but to send them on mission and ministry. The model of the book of Acts comes into play and the mission is found in the realities that because of the presence of the Holy Spirit that believers have more power to do greater things than Christ and that He "sends His followers into the world."

- **Equipping Focus** – Takes seriously that the real ministers and missionaries are those believers in the pews who stand in need of "equipping for the work" of ministry in the church and in the world. The Ephesians 4 equipping model comes from the image of "mending nets." The skills and ministry of the laity are to restore brokenness, pain, hurt and alienation from God. The professional clergy are the "equippers" to help restore the hurt, brokenness among the lay ministers and empower, unleash and equip them to "comfort others and minister to others in need of comfort and ministry."

- **Discipleship Focus** – Takes seriously the only mandate the church has "to go and make disciples" found in the Great Commission and the Great Commandment. The staff here seeks to help believers and non-believers who are spiritually thirsty inside and outside the church to move toward greater maturity in their knowledge of and experience with God through Christ. Again, the staff here invest in a few — the remnant — seeks to grow them in Christ and to lead them to reproduce healthy believers through their callings, giftings and ministries.

- **Team Focus** – This team acknowledges the diversity of callings, giftings and ministries of the body of Christ, but also acknowledges the common mission and function. That through the diversity and learning to work in harmony with each other the mission of Christ in the church and the world can be accomplished. This staff functions as team — does what needs to be done in a crises (whether in their ministry description or not), but more often than not they work from their calling and unique gifting, in cooperation with others who are uniquely gifted, on a common project or mission. The model of this staff focus then births lay ministry teams following the same model.

New Configurations: Part-time, Bi-Vocational, Volunteer, Church Grown, Adjuncts, Partnerships on Multiple Sites

The changing landscape of our world and church seems to allow new configuration for staffing churches.

- **Part-time staff** are emerging from churches of all sizes. People who are retiring early looking for a way to invest their lives offer alternative staffing options for many churches. These lay persons, professionally trained in a variety of disciplines, and who have a deep faith, are candidates for part-time positions. The person has an opportunity for a ministry of significance in the second half of life and the church benefits from their skills without having to pay full benefits. The church then provides for training at teaching churches, specialized classes and coaching by pastor or full-time staff. These part-time staff can be custodial, ministry assistants (who can even work from their home offices rather than the church having to prepare office space onsite).

- **Bi-Vocational staff** have been around for a long time, but they are finding a greater place of significance in Kingdom work these days. Because church life and Christianity have been bashed in the media we are having to earn the respect of those in the world before we can share our message. Bi-vocational staff help build this bridge. Bi-Vocational staff can be bridge-builders creating a ministry for the church through their vocation in the world. For instance if your church wants to reach children and youth, maybe your minister to youth families can be a person from the public school system or the community recreation leagues. Or if you want to reach senior adults or people with aging parents then maybe your part-time, bi-vocational staff person to spear head this could also work within the field of geronotology, nursing homes, social service field, etc.

- **Volunteer staff** are an increasing group in churches of all sizes. These are usually retired persons, or persons who work from home, or

  who are seeking for opportunities to share their gifts. This is akin to the ministry of elders in some churches where these volunteer, called, gifted believers are commissioned to shepherd, care for and give pastoral leadership to a segment of the congregation. For instance a volunteer staff person might be your minister of small groups or to families of preschoolers, or to School Teachers/ Administrators or to the medical community or to the business population in your area. Yes, these are new ministry designations emerging among volunteers, but full-time positions as well. See the outward, mission focus? It is important to ask for believers to consider this calling to in their lives and to prepare the church organization to resource and accept such a ministry. Certainly these staff need to be affirmed, recognized, resourced and celebrated like all or maybe even more frequently than other full-time staff.

- **Church grown staff** rather than seminary trained staff are increasing as well. Churches with well defined core values, targeting effective ministry in an unchurched culture find that persons groomed in their own church life make the best leaders. For most seminary trained persons, while having a good theological education, are usually greatly deficient in practical ministry skills that are effective in a church culture. Most seminaries are still training clergy as if we were living and ministering in a modern and church culture. In most situations I know of this model works very effectively, but does offer unique challenges and needs for coaching and remedial work on theological concepts needed for their ministry.

- **Adjunct staff** are emerging in situations where a unique skill set is needed over an extended, yet short-term, time to help move staff or church forward in a given specialized area of ministry. Usually this is a contractual agreement between a church consultant, seminary professor, author or other skilled professional. This agreement allows for specialized coaching or leadership without the full economic or management responsibilities over a long period of time. The success is that you get expert leadership from a reputable person from the outside who can challenge and work the system to move forward and the existing leaders don't have to catch the flack usually encountered during change.

- **Partnerships** between a group of local churches (of same or different denominations) who employ a full or part-time clergy person to target a particular group and to facilitate a partnership ministry within rural or suburban communities. Usually these are small single-staff churches. They discover they can network to find guidance

for their ministries and not have to face the full economic or super-
visory requirements alone. This usually works best with a
cooperative leadership team working with and for this partnership.

Accountability: Evaluating Success and Effectiveness in a Postmodern World

To put any staff in place and insure effectiveness new standards of
success, accountability and evaluation must be fashioned in light of
postmodern world we live in. In days gone by we made everyone
accountable the pastor or to a deacon group or personnel committee.
The persons they supervised were usually evaluated by church culture
standards:

• How many came to the programs?
• How much money was collected or sent to missions?
• How big our church buildings were?

These were not really very effective in a church culture, they are
certainly NOT effective in this secular post-modern world. Let me
make a few suggestions for you to consider:

• Evaluation and standards should be built from the primary focus of
the staff not the traditions of days gone by. For instance, if the focus
is disciplemaking then each staff should be give account for the
number of persons they consistently disciple and give evidence of
the progress that person(s) is making in following Christ.

• Evaluation should certainly acknowledge the secular, busy world we
are in rather than condemn it. For instance rather than condemning
leaders who will not serve all year in a church program, staff can give
account of the number of persons (new and established persons)
they involve in short-term project focused teams to help the church
accomplish its objectives. This helps with assimilation, development
of leadership pool and acknowledges the real challenges of persons
in a busy world. It also opens the possibility of including non-
churched, community persons in some short-term projects as an

entry point for them into relationships with church leaders. See the difference!

• Accountability should also involve persons, other than immediate supervisor, to give evidence of the discipling, mission or leadership skill of the staff persons. In other words how does his/her target audience/constituency evaluate his/her effectiveness? For instance, let's say the focus is discipleship. Could the immediate supervisor have a fellowship time for all those in the discipleship group and dialogue about how they have grown in Christ, fruit of the Spirit, discovering gifts, callings, etc. This is a great time of celebration, affirmation and planning for next steps.

• Provide opportunities for the Body of Christ to speak, to assess and to celebrate. These might even replace or become part of your regular business meeting. Focus on the mission, let those who have been discipled, been on mission, discovered their ministries share their stories. Let this be a tool of accountability, celebration, evaluation and affirmation for the staff and the other ministers God is using in your midst.

See all of this really can be, should be fun, fulfilling and challenging! Let me encourage you to consider your staff, your mission, your church's mission and calling. How can be most effective? Fulfilled? And accountable? I hope the following summary chart is helpful as you rethink staffing for your church, association, denomination or judicatory.

Discovering Church Staff That Can Function in a Postmodern Culture (Suggested Indicators for Readiness and Effectiveness)

Objective: To provide some guidelines for assessing possible candidates for staff positions in churches, associations, denominations or judicatories that are aspiring to minister effectively in a postmodern culture.

Recognize Their Spirit

• Spiritual Health

- Sense of call
- Commitment to Disciplemaking
- Openness to Spirit's leading
- Compassionate, sensitive
- Cooperative Spirit
- Authentic/Genuine
- Transparent
- Encouragers
- Knowledge of and ability to articulate ones calling, giftedness and life purpose/goals

Clarify Their Work Styles

- Coaching
- Modeling
- Mentoring
- Team Players
- Self Starters
- Consensus Builders
- Equippers
- Leaders
- Team Builder
- Facilitation skills
- Multi-tasking

Clarify Their Philosophy of Ministry/Church

- Hospital for Sinners or Hotel for Saints?
- Equipper of lay persons for ministry
- Church on Mission in the world
- Institution or Outpost for missions?
- Giftedness
- Calling

Assess Contextualizing Skills for Ministry

- Ability to read the culture
- Ability to contextualize the Good News to various cultures/people groups

- Openness to learning
- Risk Taker
- Team Builder
- Exegete scripture and culture
- Relational
- Innovative and creative in building bridges of relationship
- Knows how to help others birth new ministries (Midwife skills)
- Understanding of and skilled use of media and technology in ministry
- Listening skills

Determine Their Strategies for Disciplemaking

- Midwife birthing skills for those involved in developing personal ministries
- Invest in a core group of persons they are discipling
- Willing to be accountable and practice accountability with leaders
- Consistent and obvious evidence of prayer life and reflection
- Ongoing Bible study and ability to integrate into daily life
- Consistent involvement in discipling others and taking risks to touch the unchurched in our culture as well as walking with those

Reframing Hints To Ponder

- Find the right person and provide needed training
- Find the right person then prepare a gift based, call based ministry description
- Seek persons with the needed spirit rather than skills
- Engage a person to help your church carry out its discerned vision of ministry
- Require and resource ongoing continuing education for your ministry team

committed believers seeking a closer walk with Christ and a ministry

New Member Ministry Can Change Your Church

With the rapid pace of change in our culture comes the challenge to bring about some significant changes in many of our churches in order that the Good News might be clearly communicated to a new culture. How to make these changes, without compromising the Gospel or losing established faithful members, is a growing challenge among many church leaders. While there are many avenues to bring about change, one of the most certain avenues of effective change is to develop a healthy and effective new member ministry in your church for every age group. Let me suggest some basic principles you want to include in such a plan. The plans are certain to vary, but the principles will likely remain constant as we move into the twenty-first century.

Principles for an Effective Ministry to New Members

• **Create convenient and comfortable entry points for new members** while trying to reach persons for Christ and church membership from a secular culture the traditional church is challenged to create places of entry into relationships and church functions. These entry points must be convenient and comfortable for the newcomer; language they relate to and understand, dress that is comfortable, a relational and inviting atmosphere is essential in most cultures. What might be unique in your situation?

For example, if you trying to attract young couples with children you might consider the following to create such entry points: Where are the couples in the life stage? Age of children? Proximity to extended family? Spiritual foundations? Who are the couples? Children? Are they native to the area? Education level? Professions/careers? Interests/hobbies?

You might discover that an adopt a grandparent emphasis might be an entry point, or maybe a MOPS program for Mothers of Preschool Children, or maybe a support group for dual career marriages, or the sponsoring of a little league team or Girl or Boy Scout troops. What entry points do you see?

The creation of these entry points helps change a traditional church's structure and organization to be more friendly to strangers and newcomers to church and Baptist traditions.

• **Create a community atmosphere among the newcomers** by networking them together across vocational lines, hobbies, ages of children, caregivers of aging parents, etc. and seek to build family/supportive relationships among the newcomers themselves. Such a community is certain to help you retain them.

Research tells us that newcomers into your church need to know six people by name in less than 6 months or they are not likely to be faithful in their participation.

Such community can be built in banquet settings, backyard fellowships or affinity clusters at the pastor/staff or deacons' homes. It might be done at lunch or during an intentional vacation time among families. It might be a retreat or in a chat room on the Internet. Someone needs to facilitate the learning of information among newcomers by asking non-threatening questions — favorite colors, place, food, animal, vacation spot, etc.; to the more personal questions like: favorite memory of childhood, most embarrassing moment, time you felt God's presence most strongly. Consistency of contact is important in building community.

The building of these relational networks and communities helps focus the church on those outside the "inner circle of leadership/membership" and helps generate community-building experiences for each age group.

•**Provide a meaningful opportunity to learn the history and vision of the church**. This might happen even before they join the church — as an inquirers class, video or audio cassette or even a website. Remember to ask them what they are hearing, what questions are being generated and how they feel about what they are learning. Pay attention, these are real community building questions and opportunities.

You might also include some persons from the established church to help you communicate the personal history of the church. This provides a way for bridge building between the newcomers and the established members. This is essential for trust-building that must occur if leadership is to be shared with newcomers as they come to understand the church's mission and discover their giftings and callings as members of the Body of Christ. The bridge-building efforts help facilitate a clarifying of or a changing of values of the newcomers or the existing church.

• **Focus on a personal relationship with God and not just denominational or church mechanics** is paramount for a new member ministry. People are spiritually thirsty in today's secular culture, but most are not looking for denominational or church issues, they are looking for a relationship with God. How can you create such experiences for each age group of newcomers and/or new members? Could the affinity groups be guided to reflect on daily life experiences in light of their belief systems and the framework of Christian theology?

Asking the following questions might help facilitate this dialogue:

• Where have you experienced or seen God at work in the last six months?
• How would you describe your most powerful spiritual experience?
• How do you open yourself to the work and power of God?

Focusing on developing a personal relationship with God will help focus the person and the church on God and not on what man can do. It will likely help open us up to the power and presence of God in a life rather than just what the church might do for them or what they might do for the church. When one becomes connected strongly to God all else falls into place. Such a personal conversation and focus will ultimately make strong suggestions to those who plan for Christian education and worship in your congregation.

As we enter the twenty-first century it will be increasingly important to teach our church leaders and members the importance of an

Reframing Hints To Ponder

• Doing an effective job in new member training is a way to change a church culture in three to five years.
• Creating comfortable non-threatening entry points for new members is essential.
• Creating community among newcomers helps assimilate and keep them when they can't "get into" the established church community.

effective ministry to new members. Such a ministry is critical for the established church and to insure the birthing of a new church that will effectively communicate the biblical truths so a new generation might understand and receive Christ. If you want to change your church in any way, the investment in developing an effective new member ministry is worthy of your time, energy and resources. Will you take the challenge? You only need a plan and one newcomer or new member to begin!

Roadmap for Birthing Personal Ministries

While the birthing of personal ministries comes forth from the individual believer, the corporate body of the church has a vitally important responsibility too. The church calls forth the ministry, creates the permission-giving atmosphere for the ministry to be birthed and creates a variety of opportunities to nurture the believer and the ministry. How does this manifest itself? The church plays a vital and multifaceted role in the birthing and developing of personal ministries. Below is an overview of some critical roles for you to explore through other reading and research:

- *Nurturer* – every aspect of new life needs to be nurtured. Desiring the presence of the new, nurturing rather than resisting its presence and celebrating the newness it creates among the old.
- *Accountability* – that the new will move the work of God forward. This is likely not to happen in familiar ways, since it's new, but the corporate body needs to hold high the Biblical mandate, not necessarily the historical or traditional venues, for the work of the people of God.
- *Authenticate/Validate* – it's critically important to validate the birthing of the new and to celebrate the calling and gifting of the believer birthing the new. Maybe a commissioning service, maybe a part of the corporate budget, maybe an opportunity to share the dream with others and enlist their support/help. There are a number of churches whose biggest event of the year is a celebration of all the personal ministries of their members. It is often called a Ministry

Celebration. All involved in personal ministries have an opportunity to celebrate and share their joy. What an exciting time this is.

• *Money follows Mission* is a rule of church life that I've seen manifest many times. When people become excited about, involved in and find meaning in doing missions their commitment to financing the dreams and ministries follow.

These are only a few thoughts to get you started. Let me encourage you to pray, seek God's calling and gifting in your life and to celebrate that which He chooses to do through you regardless of how odd, how untraditional it might be. Remember He called Abraham and Sarah in their eighties, He called Moses, a man who stuttered, to lead a people from captivity, fisherman to join his inner circle and they changed the world! What's He calling you to be/do?

While the challenges seem overwhelming and insurmountable we can find hope in those pioneers who are discovering ways of discipling in a secular culture. Let's turn to practical ideas and models that are emerging. Discipleship that matters in an unchurched culture touches values, organizations, leadership expectations, curriculum and evangelism/outreach strategies.

Notes

[1] Tom Sine, *Mustard Seed Vs. McWorld: Reinventing Life and Faith for the Future* (Grand Rapids MI: Baker Books, 1999), 136.

[2] Lyle Schaller, *44 Steps Up Off the Plateau* (Nashville: Abingdon Press, 1993), 42-46.

[3] Some resources to help in this transition include the following: *Outgrowing an Ingrown Church* by John Miller; *Transitioning a Church* by Dan Southerland; *Making the Church Work* by Edward Hammett, and *Revolution in Leadership* by Reggie McNeal. Another resource is *Sharing Christ Meeting Needs* by Don Atkinson and Charles Roeselle.

[4] Richard Jones, "Learning to Follow the Holy Spirit," *Net Results* (March 2001), 12-13.

[5] Adapted from Rick Richardson, *Evangelism Outside the Box* (Downers Grove IL: Intervarsity Press, 2000).

[6] George Barna, Workbook from the "Re-churching the Unchurched" Seminar, Charlotte, NC (18 March 2001) , 4.

[7] Ibid., 27-28.

[8] "Gray's the Color of Life," <http://www.gospel.com.net/guide/gray-matrix.html>.

[9] McCloskey, Mark and Bill Bright. "An Interpersonal Communication Model: The Engel Scale Explained," from *Tell It Often, Tell It Well* (Here's Life Publishers, 1985), ch. 17.

Discipleship That Matters in an Unchurched Culture

Walking into Fear Discerning the Spirit

I have been a Southern Baptist all my life. I've been a Christian since 12 years of age. During all this time I've found myself intricately involved in the life of a local church. Participating in Sunday School, Discipleship Training, mission training and involvement. From this I quickly found myself in various leadership positions in these same organizations and serving on countless committees. You might say I was "a good Baptist." I was faithful and most would say effective in all of these arenas of church life.

The organizations provided various forums for my leaders and mentors to instruct me in the faith and to guide me in life. During the 1950s and again in the early 1970s all this seemed to work fairly well. However during the meantime in my early college days I had a crisis of faith, as do most students, where I started to question the effectiveness of what we were busy doing. I worked harder and longer, prayed more, talked to others more, and involved myself in many hands on ministry experiences. What I quickly realized was that working harder, and longer and praying more wasn't necessarily improving my effectiveness.

Such a crisis led me to study Scripture for myself, to assess my growth in Christ and my effectiveness in terms of fulfilling the Great Commission and the purpose for which I felt God had created me. Let me telescope time and struggle to say that I realized that much of what I was involving myself in was primarily church work and not the work of the Church. I also realized that I was probably a good Baptist, but I was not a good fruit bearing and fulfilled Christian. I was busy doing church, going to meetings, but I was not actively engaged in a personal relationship with a personal Christ. When I shared this with most of my fellow church members they didn't understand, nor were they even open to considering that I felt much of what I /we were involved with was basically a stumbling block to the purposes of the kingdom of God rather than an active part of our calling to that kingdom. I felt we were interested in making good churchpersons more than we were interested in growing impacting Christians.

I titled this section "Walking into Fear Discerning the Spirit" for three reasons: 1) Such reality and skill formation is what got me out of my introverted and self-serving behaviors and attitudes; 2) Such are the skills I'm facing again as I work on this manuscript — for I realize I'm challenging the status quo and for many the core of what church is and what church is about; 3) These are the primary skills Christian educators must learn to teach and grow in those of us seeking to be Christian in an increasingly secular world. In the 1950s and 1960s we were to some degree still part of a church culture and the system (curriculum, literature, and organization) we had still "worked." After the 1960s passed with all of the new freedoms, secularity and "God is dead" campaigns skepticism grew and new deeper more personal needs emerged and the effectiveness of church began to decline.

The skepticism and newness of needs snowballed and most church leaders just worked harder at what we were already doing — believing that because it had been working, simply doing more of it would suffice. But it didn't. Now the church faces growing secularization of society, the accusations that there is little if any difference between the churched and the unchurched persons and a growing irrelevance to most persons in our communities.

I've spent the last 15 plus years learning to walk into my fear and learning to watch and follow the Spirit's leading. Many of my colleagues trivialize my ideas or declare my accusations about the ineffectiveness of most of what we do as "stirring up trouble." I've been made to feel at times as a traitor among Southern Baptists. For I wanted to follow "a new fresh wind blowing" that I discerned as the

Spirit's leading and it seemed to go against "the traditional directions of church." So I was challenged to walk into my fears. For you see, I was a people pleaser. I wanted people to like me and when I didn't go with them I wasn't embraced — in fact I was "black balled" by some. They would say, "let's don't invite Eddie to this meeting he'll do nothing but sidetrack us and stir up trouble."

Fortunately God has provided persons all along my journey who would embrace, encourage and give permission to walk into my fears, explore places off the map; dream new dreams and try new experiments. These persons have been my lifelines in the Christian faith and certainly in church and denominational work. Without the few that God strategically placed in my paths I may have left the church all together. I don't want to be part of the problem any longer; I want to be part of the solution. My calling is to work within the system to refresh it — restore it — upgrade it to be more effective in our changing culture. Let me confess it's this calling that has kept me going on many occasions for the journey is tough, long and filled with trappings in the most unlikely places.

Leadership Lessons

I've had to learn leadership lessons from Moses, Abraham, Jeremiah, Paul, David, and Jesus to keep moving and be faithful to my calling. Moses didn't want to lead, he didn't feel he had the gifts or skills to lead, but he overcame the doubts and followed God's inner urgings. He didn't feel worthy to lead because of his own shortcomings. Moses was to lead grumbling, self-centered and self-serving people who wanted to cling to the familiar rather than venture into a new land. He kept his ear to the voice of God and his heart to learning obedience and his eye on the Promised Land.

Abraham and his wife were called to move from the familiar and comfortable to go to a place he knew not of. He had to learn that God was not calling him to give him a blessing, but rather to make him a blessing (Gen 12) He didn't understand or even agree with God's ideas, but he worked to be faithful to what he saw and heard.

Jeremiah was a young guy with opinions and ideas different from those in his frame of reference. He wasn't always popular or tactful in communicating what he saw in his heart, but his persevering helped birth a new and more faithful people of God.

Paul, a Jew, who was called to minister to the Gentiles, faced many cultural challenges we face today. Called to minister to persons that the religious people condemned or judged and learning to become "all things to all men that he might save some" has been a challenge and guide for me at times when I watched the church focus on "us" rather than trying to reach "them."

David, "a man after God's own heart," but also a man who had his own failures in life. Yet David was a strong leader used by God. The scars of his life became the fuel for much of his ministry. Embracing and letting God work through pain is an ongoing lesson for us all.

Jesus, the man who found power not in a king's scepter but a servant's towel, challenges the CEO model of leadership that is so popular in today's culture. His sensitivity and openness to his Father's voice encourages me. His faithfulness to move beyond the norm in order to move the Kingdom forward offers hope, help and role modeling.

Walking into Fears

Enough of my personal journey in the past, now for the present. I realize that places in this manuscript are going to threaten the traditional organizations and philosophy of Christian education for some. I realize that even the thought of change in the context of most churches is an ugly thought that doesn't deserve enough attention to even talk about it. We simply say, "things are going okay now, let's don't rock the boat," or the deep reality of the apathy and introversion of our church leads us to declare, "we have to take care of ourselves before we can worry about those outside the church." I believe both comments grieve the heart of God and enable the growing dysfunction and ineffectiveness of a church.

Such attitudes are not in every church — thank God — but they are in many churches because I've been in those churches and believe me they would rather die than change. Walking into fears means confronting this reality and deciding not to be an enabler of the dysfunction or ineffectiveness and working to lead the people out of the wilderness, to encounter Christ in a secular world or to break through traditions that Kingdom purposes are accomplished. It is risky leadership. It calls for a transformed leader who is:

- Sensitive to the Spirit's leadership
- Aware of giftedness and calling
- Discerning of timing and of people
- Passionate about the biblical mission of the church

Discerning the leadership of the Holy Spirit is crucial and yet many believers and leaders are poorly skilled and rehearsed in this skill. Let me simply outline discernment as I've come to understand and experience it. When I started trusting the discernment process many of the pieces of this manuscript became real to me.

- Prayer is of utmost importance. Learning to be in a spirit of prayer but also committing time and energy to prayer is essential.
- Gathering of all possible evidence or information in order to make best-informed decisions.
- Learning to look for confirmations within you, the community of faith and external confirmations. Recognizing patterns, synchronization of events and circumstances. Discovering God's hidden activity in taking the next step and moving beyond your fears.
- Learning to ask and recognize where the Spirit is and where the Spirit's preceded us are critical. Learning to assess where things seem to be in harmony and where there seems to be a dis-ease.
- Discernment also involves exploring potential, possibilities and place for the "true self" to emerge. The difference between our "false self" and our "true self" often activates discernment.

We can't avoid counting the cost when it comes to discernment. Discerning the movement of God often calls us not only to move from our fears but also to move to places that are unknown and to know and experience that God goes before us. My friends often remind me that there is more in the New Testament about "knowing the will of God" than "doing the will of God." Such discerning skills are in constant refinement and use for effective leaders.

It seems to me that reframing Christian education for the twenty-first century calls leaders to consider change of self, a reinventing of oneself and/or organizations, philosophy and infrastructure. Such reframing often challenges us to learn to live in and through pain and to live in ambiguity as the new is being birthed and the old is fading away. Being open to such exploration and consideration is essential to moving out of the wilderness of ineffectiveness and apathy. Leaders who are closed to exploring such possibilities might be preserving a tradition (that has worked in days gone by) but they may be preventing the birth of something new God desires. Confronting such leaders and values calls for leaders to walk into their fears and move by the Spirit.

Understanding the Nature and Scope of Leadership

Leadership is a key issue in moving the functions of the church forward in the twenty-first century. Without leaders that have learned how and are committed to walk by faith and not be derailed by fear, most churches are stuck. Greg Morris overviews some critical concepts about leaders in the October 16, 2000 issue of his e-newsletter, *Leadership Dynamics*:

- Leadership is not a position. Leadership is more than a title or rank. Almost anyone can be elected, selected, anointed, self-appointed, promoted or succeeded. Christian leaders should be certain that their goal is to serve God and others, not to receive the title or honor that comes with leadership.
- Leadership is not building a personality cult. "Leadership is not magnetic personality. It is not making friends and influencing people; that is flattery. Leadership is lifting a person's vision to higher sights, the raising of a person's performance to higher standards, the building of a personality beyond its normal limitations." (Peter Drucker)
- Leadership is not being indispensable. Some leaders build followers, while others build leaders. The mark of a true leader is demonstrated by the fact that the show must and can go on without him or her. As David Watson wisely observed, "A Christian who is ambitious to be a star disqualifies himself as a leader."

- Leadership is not about blaming others. Leadership is first and foremost being honest and responsible for the decisions you make or fail to make.
- Leadership is not privilege. In recent days we have witnessed "leaders" using their position for personal or financial gain at the expense of the organization or ministry they lead. Leaders will not use their position for their own advantage or comfort and should not ask others to do what they are unwilling to do themselves.

All too often churches have valued leadership in positions filled rather than callings acted upon and gifts used. Today's challenges are calling for strong leaders with a vision. Let me illustrate by introducing you to several leaders that are moving through their fears as they watch God birth new things in and through and around them because of their obedience.

I first met Charlie about five years ago when I did a workshop at a Baptist church. He's a 70-year-old deacon, long-time member of this church, and at one time part of the "old guard" of the church now being transformed from the inside out. Through some of the mirroring activities used during that seminar, Charlie faced the hard facts of his dying Barraca Men's Sunday School Class and the stagnancy of his beloved congregation. He became increasingly aware of the changing face of their community. Such insight became a source of change in Charlie's heart. I've stayed in touch with Charlie through the years and have been blessed to watch God do a work of transformation. Charlie is now raising money to begin a SOS (Serve Our Savior) ministry in downtown Winston-Salem, NC. This will be an interdenominational opportunity for persons to serve Christ and reach out to the poorest of the poor. Not only is he leading this effort, he is working with local communication professionals and his church to begin a group for those the SOS teams touch who might want to explore the Christian faith in a nonthreatening, comfortable environment. He's shifting his focus from the Barraca class to the SOS group. I'm confident God has a hand on Charlie. He's thirsty and hungry for direction, support and equipping for this new ministry.

Jena, a young owner of a local skating rink in a rural mountain community, came to me after a workshop and said, with tears in her eyes, "I know what God wants me to do through my skating rink but I need some help." She had connected that her faith life and her vocational life were connecting. She had a burden for all the unchurched kids and families that frequented her skating rink each week. She is a strong leader there to keep peace among her energy filled patrons. They have an earned respect of her. She's now looking for traction for her new journey. What can be done to help her in this journey of birthing a new ministry?

David, a young man recently divorced after seven years of marriage, is working to find healing and meaning in a traumatic and painful divorce and custody battle. His wife had an affair at work and manifests signs of not only codependent behavior, but also manic depression. After going to their pastor and church for help, he found little assistance. Prayers were offered and appreciated, but he and their entire family needed ministry that wasn't present in the churches where they had been members. Now David understands, through a local counselor and much reading and dialogue with others outside his church, that his pain is a pathway to his ministry. He wants to begin

Reframing Hints To Ponder

- Working harder and longer and praying more wasn't necessarily improve my effectiveness in ministry.
- I felt we were interested in making good churchpersons more than we were interested in growing impacting Christians.
- Now the church faces growing secularization of society.
- I've had to learn leadership lessons from Moses, Abraham, Jeremiah, Paul, David, and Jesus.
- Discerning the leadership of the Holy Spirit is crucial and yet many believers and leaders are poorly skilled and rehearsed in this skill.
- Discerning the movement of God often calls us not only to move from our fears but also to move to places that are unknown and to know and experience that God goes before us.
- Leadership is a key issue in moving the functions of the church forward in the twenty-first century.
- Learning to birth ministries and how to become an incubator for new ministries is a challenge for today's and tomorrow's leaders and churches.

a ministry to persons inside the church who are facing divorce. How can we coach him in this new Christian journey?

God is birthing many new ministries, through many different venues and for many different people groups than most churches have been targeting. While the ministries based inside the church walls still have great significance and need for effective training, the new ministries are often outside traditional structures and organizations. Such ministries need a different set of training, resourcing, supporting experiences. How does a church equip persons for such ministries? How do you walk with them and guide them through fears and into balanced and effective leadership. What does an equipping church look like? How does it differ from a traditional program-based church?

Spiritual Formation: Its Shapes, Sounds, and Structures

Having tried to make the argument that since our culture is primarily a post-Christian and postmodern world and that the focus of Christian education will move beyond a centralized, curricula and teacher driven approach many ask what will it look like. There are many churches who arc doing a great job in their spiritual formation ministry in this secular age. Let me express my appreciation to them for their pioneering efforts in this journey.

Christian Education or Spiritual Formation Experiences?

While Christian education has served us well in a church culture, the time is here for us to consider a ministry of spiritual formation. The reason for the shift is more than terminology. It has to do with focus and the people we are trying to reach. While there is an all time high interest in spirituality in our culture, there's not much interest in Christian education. Can we take the interest in spirituality and create nonthreatening entry points genuinely designed to help them explore their spiritual formation from where they are, not where we might want them to be? Can we do this without forsaking our Christian commitments or convictions, while at the same time abandoning some of the methodologies, structures, or language that might be building barriers instead of bridges with those we are called to reach?

The vast diversity of belief systems, rituals, traditions, family systems, family values, and cultural groups offer much challenge to most dimensions of our society. The challenge is present for the Church as well. Spiritual formation is a concern of many persons in these diverse groups. I've learned that spiritual formation is not about teaching someone to parrot religious language but to help them embrace life transforming truths. Spiritual formation is about helping persons connect with God — to discover God at work in daily life and to join God in His work in and through the individual. How might we create experiences that will help nurture persons forward? Asking these questions might help us learn from each other's journey and create support systems that would nurture the journey rather than hinder the journey.

In my area of North Carolina we have available to us many multicultural events and experiences, yet I've noted in very few of them is religion or spirituality issues a part of that learning and sharing experience in focused kind of ways. Certainly it is integrated in much of the art, dance, music, crafts and language, but why couldn't a spiritual formation experience be created to facilitate sharing and learning? What might it look like? How might it be fashioned to be more effective in the culture of the twenty-first century?

The Effective Church in the 21st Century

Many church leaders often see trying to envision the future as a useless task. Many leaders suggest that "only God knows the future," others indicate that "life is changing so rapidly no one can keep up," still others suggest that "the church needs to hold on to the past and not worry about the future." While there might be a kernel of truth in each position the reality of today is that many persons are unchurched and some of us who are members of the church feel the church is increasingly irrelevant. The challenge of the church of the twenty-first century is how to become relevant in a secular culture and how can we be effective in handling, communicating and sharing with integrity, the Good News in a pluralistic and secular culture.

Effectiveness in the Past

Effectiveness and success of the church in the last several decades has been attached to programs, buildings, budgets and bodies. How many persons are we reaching, teaching, preaching to, or baptizing? How many persons do we have on our church staff? Others measure success by how much money are we collecting? How much are we giving to missions? Still others say we are successful when we build bigger and better buildings to house our worship, education, recreational or ministry needs. Then there are those persons, who basically grew up in church in the last 30 to 40 years, who assess a church's effectiveness by the number of programs the church offers to its parishioners. Some even call these our "five star churches" — churches with missions programs for men and women, Sunday School, Discipleship Training, and worship.

When these numbers begin to drop most churches blame the pastor/staff and assume no responsibility for the eroding themselves. Most churches are pastor/staff driven in that they are blamed when things aren't going well. They also seem to gather the affirmations when things are going well. I'm certainly not minimizing the leadership roles of pastor/staff. I am suggesting that those leadership roles are equally as important as those in the volunteer leadership pool. Building an effective, balanced and caring team of leaders is essential in growing an effective church in any day.

Effectiveness in the 21st Century

While numbers of persons touched and reached will still be wholesome indicators they will certainly not be the primary indicators for the effective church in the 21st century. Numbers are important and they do represent people, however our counting needs to reflect a different perspective and acknowledge the realities of our day. For instance, in a secular culture, we need to count not just how many people *come to* our church services, but count how many persons *leave our services and go* into the world and make a difference for Christ. Knowing that it is increasingly difficult for unchurched persons to find their way into our traditional church services, we might need to count how many non-threatening, comfortable entry points we are

89

creating to reach the unchurched. That non-threatening environment will be increasingly important and will take on very non-traditional times, foci and groupings. (For additional measurement guidelines see my *The Gathered and Scattered Church*.)

Reframing Effectiveness for the 21st Century Church

The realities of the twenty-first century challenge the reframing for the twenty-first century church. Dual career marriages, single parent families, blended families, multicultural families and communities, time-poor parents, persons working from home, technology, economic shifts, changing role of women, the information explosion, the growing minority status of WASP (white Anglo-Saxon Protestants) and the increase in Hispanics, Afro-Americans and Asians and the 24/7 (twenty-four hour day, seven days a week) time frame of life. These represent only a few of the major challenges and shifts in our culture. Trying to hold on to the "good old days" will only lead your church to the grave for the days of the past will never be again. Our society and culture have changed. In light of these and other changes how does the church thrive in this culture without compromising the Good News? Paul gave some helpful guidelines in Romans 12. Allow me to use his thoughts to reframe our transition from centralized approach to Christian education to a decentralized and centralized approach to spiritual formation.

Reframing Hints To Ponder

Be not conformed to this world (as you've known it)....Focus on people groups not programs

- Focus on spiritual condition of people being reached or targeted rather than conversion
- Focus on spiritual journey rather than church membership
- Focus on walking with, rather than just telling or converting
- Focus on growth celebrations rather than just conversion celebrations (rites of passage)
- Focus on telling and re-telling the stories rather than just telling the story

Be ye transformed by the renewing of your mind. Focus on relationships and life experiences not preserving traditions

- Create entry points rather than just enlisting into existing classes/programs.
- Create Christ-honoring relationships rather than passive relationships.
- Create growth celebrations rather than just conversion celebrations (rites of passage).
- Create learning experiences rather than just teaching forums.
- Create affinity groups rather than just teaching classes.

What It Looks Like in Real Life

Now for instance, how might this translate into our multicultural festivals in North Carolina? Could someone serve as a catalyst in our multicultural festivals for this learning adventure and ask the planning group for the multicultural event if a spiritual formation dialogue/planning group could work together? This group could begin to function as a small group, building relationships, and sharing beliefs and discussing how we could help persons understand each other's beliefs in more effective ways. Might there be a time of fellowship with each other during worship or dialogue, maybe by creating a book club to share some of each other's literature as a pathway of spiritual formation. What about a time of interpretation or translating of each other's art, dance or worship styles? Maybe we could be guests of each other's worship and educational events. Such partnership is likely to build bridges rather than more barriers.

The Shapes of Spiritual Formation

The ministry of spiritual formation will likely take many shapes. Let me recall some of those vital ingredients discovered in the early church in the book of Acts. Spiritual formation experiences will likely be built around these elements:

• Relational
• Flexible and spontaneous
• Focused on life issues
• Based in authenticity
• An intentional search for truth and wholeness
• Decentralized more often than not
• Propelled by theological reflection & story
• Nurtured by reflection on story & multimedia challenges
• Rooted in truth
• Life-transforming

While these are catalytic elements for spiritual formation in a secular age, there are still other possible shapes, that might be considered unconventional to the traditional church leader. Some of the shapes or structures — avenues for possible spiritual formation — might include:

• Book Clubs – in bookstores, coffee shops, community buildings or homes
• Self-Help Groups – where the entry point focuses on helping persons with personal pain around personal issues. These groups are likely to meet in places other than the church.
• Business clubs – places for building relationships, sharing humanitarian interest with others and possibly being a catalyst for a productive spiritual formation dialogue.

- Chat rooms on the internet
- Websites designed for theological reflection on various life experiences
- Media events
- Community-based drama and music teams
- Storyteller in children's bookstores or community events
- Affinity clubs for defined interest groups or people groups
- Hands on ministry/mission teams
- Sports teams in the church or community
- Vacationer's club

These are simply illustrative, and to many from a strong church culture background you are asking how in the world are these things going to help teach people the Bible, introduce people to Christ or get them to become member of my church? These are valid concerns, however remember in an unchurched culture the objective is to move them forward in their faith formation. Think of each of the above and ask yourself or planning group:

- How can we intentionally utilize these experiences, where unchurched people might be found, as a spiritual formation experience?
- How can we equip some believers to be active catalysts for spiritual formation in these experiences?
- What would make these experiences an effort that moves the learner forward in their faith development?
- By what standards will we measure the effectiveness of the learner's role or the spiritual formation experience?

The Sounds of Spiritual Formation

In a postmodern culture that is visually and digitally driven, technologically savvy, and a product of a "sound bite world" the sounds of spiritual formation must be considered. What do I mean by sounds of spiritual formation?

- What is it that the learner is hearing you say? Take note of the language you use and how it is being interpreted?

- What sounds are a daily part of the learner's world? Are they in a high tech world? A dysfunctional family system? What music do they listen to? What art forms capture their attention?
- What sources of the media capture the learner's attention? Are they internet users, part of an e-learning system at work or home? Are they moviegoers? What are their favorite films?

Such questions point us to tuning into the world of the learner (believer or unbeliever). In our world there is a keen awareness and utilization of various learning styles/preferences. There's an astute need of many to preserve their historic culture and rituals — many of these can be springboards for building bridges of communication of the Good News.

The Structures of Spiritual Formation — Barriers or Bridges?

When we think of Christian education structures most of us think of classes, groups, organizations, worship services, choirs, communion, baptism, ordination, and mission. While these are valuable and effective for many, they are barriers and ineffective means for many others who are not from or appreciative of a church culture.

The structures of spiritual formation for a secular culture can be best summarized biblically by the discipling model of Christ. The first phase of his disciplemaking journey was "come and see." He simply wanted to attract persons, not giving them responsibilities of leadership, or placing high standards on them or their "religious behaviors." He was creating a nonthreatening comfortable entry point[1] (See Appendix A).

John Shea, professor at the Mundelein seminary in Chicago, wrote a book some years ago in which he called Jesus "the Spirit Master" rather than a Teacher of Faith. He thus dramatized the difference between education and real teaching. He writes that education:

> suggests distance and impartiality. This involves someone who disseminates information; in this case a body of beliefs are passed along...[resulting in that] he or she has mastered some subject matter and is about the business of organizing it and passing it along. The student is a secondary object of attention. As teachers

often say with a shrug, students either "get the material or they don't."[2]

In contrast he described the teaching of Jesus:

The title 'Spirit Master' initially focuses Jesus in his capacity to engage people on the level of spirit and invite them into his own spirit. He does not teach lessons; he primarily encounters people. He is passionately person-centered. When he tells his disciples to come away with him to an out-of-the-way place, he is not only suggesting rest and relaxation (Mk 6:30). He wants time with them. Just 'being with' his disciples is an essential ingredient of his way of teaching and their way of learning. Jesus engages the total person. In modern parlance, he communicates in the context of an 'I-Thou' encounter. Certainly Jesus instructs his disciples on the level of perceptions, attitudes, and actions. In fact, our focus will be on perceptions and attitudes. But in and through this communication a deeper reality is handed on. The very spirit of Jesus is communicated. This happens through symbiosis and osmosis. They walk and talk and eat and work with Jesus; and there is a slow assimilation of how he sees and hears the world. This process is partly conscious and partly unconscious . . . Once the spirit is shared, the person of the Master lives on in the person of the disciple . . . This gives us a clue to the depth of the relationship between Jesus the master and anyone who would be his disciple. Jesus wants the disciple to experience the reality he knows; he does not want to pass along conclusions of his experience. In the deepest moment it is not a sharing of belief and theology but an introduction to Abba. If Abba is met, shared beliefs follow, flowers out of the same soil. All knowledge must be realized. Realized knowledge changes perception and overflows into action.[3]

For me this states what is wrong with most religious education as well as the direction it must take to find a Christian formation model — a rather major paradigm shift. C. Ellis Nelson, professor of religious education at Union Seminary in New York, and former president of Louisville Presbyterian Seminary, wrote: "Communication of Christian faith (especially by educational methods) means forming the mind [I would say the total person] according to tradition in such a way that persons can experience the God of that tradition and also be open to experiences which may transform the tradition itself. In short, it is a process of formation looking for the possibility of transformation."[4]

Most Sunday school programs seek to educate — memorize, moralize, master. Formation seeks to allow the biblical text to encounter the total experience of the person and transform. Robert Mulholland, professor of New Testament and Provost at Asbury Theological Seminary, describes in his acclaimed book, *Shaped By the Word: The Power of Scripture in Spiritual Formation* the almost exclusive way that Scripture has been used in the churches — to gain as much information as possible, to control and master the text, and then to analyze, criticize and evaluate the texts as valuable or not.

Contrasted is "formational reading" which is slower, seeks the life formation from the text, allows the unexpected to show up, and does not hold scripture at arms length, but experiences its penetrating power. It respects the value of informational reading, but knows that reading the text must go beyond to "break the crust of life, provide spiritual discipline, and to nurture growth."[5]

Eugene Peterson, in *Working the Angles: The Shape of Pastoral Integrity*, writes, "The intent in reading Scripture, among people of faith, is to extend the range of our listening to the God who reveals himself in word, to become acquainted with the ways in which he has spoken in various times and places, along with the way in which people respond when he speaks."[6] That process is being rediscovered in the ancient practice of lectio divina, or praying the Scripture. Groups meet weekly to share their own personal working with the Scripture passage for the week — often the lectionary reading for the coming Sunday, especially the Gospel passage. Background material that reflects good scholarship is shared in a one page written summary before the week. Then, each person is asked to spend some time daily, reading the passage, allowing the text to speak personally, and then silently to meditate on it. The personal meditations are then shared at the weekly meeting. The goal is to allow the transformative power of Scripture to be shared.

Thus Scripture study becomes formational. How then do we preserve the best of our traditions, without compromising biblical integrity and reach, shape, and mature in the faith our secular and primarily unchurched culture? Here are some clues I've found:

Some clues about effective structures for spiritual formation in a secular age:

- Multi-task — utilize the layers of one's life as avenues for spiritual formation.
- Opportunities for the gathered church – places and times for congregational gatherings for equipping and worship that are designed for worship and community building. (See my *The Gathered and Scattered Church* for additional insights.)
- Opportunities for the Scattered church — identify places, experiences and times for the scattered church to encourage and equip them to *be* salt, light and leaven. (See my *The Gathered and Scattered Church* for additional insights.)
- Multi-disciplinary — utilize variety of teaching methodologies to acknowledge diversity of learning styles, cultural preferences and sensitivity to language and spiritual formation.
- Decentralized — focusing on the life transformation 7 days a week, 24 hours a day in all arenas of life, not on the traditional meeting times, places and programs.
- Multidimensional is key. Work at spiritual formation on multiple levels simultaneously. We spend more time on various dimensions and relationships rather than on preserving institutionally based structures and programs.
- Accountability — invitation to and opportunity for accountability relationships to help move persons forward in wholeness and spiritual formation.
- Technology and media usage — creative use of technology and media to facilitate spiritual formation, learning, and accountability. Does your church have a webmaster that understands this dimension of spiritual formation? Is your church Christian education facility and organization "wired for" this approach to spiritual formation?

These shifts can be summarized by the following chart. Think through each element of the shift in light of your comfort level as a leader and consider what new skills and goals you need to move toward greater effectiveness as a believer in this secular culture.

Emerging Shifts in Organizational Principles of Christian Education

FROM	TO
Flakes Formula focus	People focused
Age graded	Affinity groups & age
At Church (centralized)	Anywhere (decentralized)
Churchmanship issues	Lifestyle issues
Print based delivery system	Media & relational delivery system
Group focused teaching	Individual & Group Peer learning
Developmental Ed. Psychology	Rites of passage around life issues/needs
Leader Driven/Focused	Learner Driven/Focused
Information Sharing	Information Management & Integration
Teaching Biblical facts	Learning/Alignment of life
Encountering Information	Experiencing Life Transformation

Getting New Concepts into Real Life

Let me try to illustrate several of these concepts in a real life situation. Years ago I realized that I didn't know any unchurched people, yet I was teaching, writing, and preaching about them. It became an intense conviction and focus of my prayer life and personal accountability. As I prayed God helped me to become aware of many unchurched people that had always been in my world; I just hadn't paid much attention or been much concerned about them. Over a period of years I became closely associated with Randy, Suzanne, Connie, Chuck, Claudia, and Marie —all unchurched for one reason or another, some non-believers, some searchers and some lost souls.

I started to listen, spend time with them and determine their life journey, struggles and dreams. Randy and I enjoyed coffee shops, reading of good books, *Oprah*, and the world of investment and retirement planning. As we shared from these common venues. I came to learn of the death of his mother when he was a preschooler. I learned of the feelings of abandonment and loss that still haunted him and were causing him to fall into unhealthy addictions to try to fill the void and pain. As he shared this struggle, Oprah Winfrey was dealing with some of those same issues on her TV talk show. That became an objective source of information we could debrief. Through emails, phone conversations, and face to face dialogues, we began to unpack some of his grief and identify a vast array of feelings he could not identify and was captive to. I prayed for him and listened very carefully for his spiritual language — for indeed he had proven he was a spiritually thirsty and hungry young man. He wanted to become whole again. He wanted release from his addictions. He wanted to break cycles of codependency. He was seeking redemption, release and a rebirth. We then stumbled across some movies that helped us unpack some new information in a nonthreatening way. All the time his trust increased, his thirst deepened with each new insight he gained, and each piece of relief he was experiencing. Randy had moved from talking about "getting into the flow of life and joining his energy with that of the universe" to speaking "of grace, mercy, new birth, forgiveness etc." I'm convinced this happened because of the relationship of trust we were building. I was learning to build bridges not barriers with unchurched persons. Randy was seeing and feeling change. He talked about me being a lifeline for him and a spiritual guide to his recovery. See, this experience is filled with redemptive, trust building experiences. We worked off of many different layers of life at one time. We used various venues for communication and spiritual formation work. The framing of my questions and the sensitivity of my heart and hearing became critical sources for Randy's new birth — a discovering of another way, a better way, God's way.

I hope this gives you a glimpse of a scattered church approach to spiritual formation with one young man. Strangely enough a group of persons emerged over time that heard of or saw Randy's progress and a small group emerged. Randy started helping others on this same journey. I'm currently apprenticing him as he tries to help others find the "living water" he has found and "release from the bondage and depression" he has experienced.

Reframing Hints To Ponder

- Christian education was a good focus for the church culture, now we must shift to a spiritual formation focus to help move an secular culture forward in faith.
- Leadership roles of pastor/staff are equally important to those of volunteers in the leadership pool.
- In a secular culture we need to count those who leave the church services and go into the world rather than just count those who come to our meetings.
- Learning to create a nonthreatening comfortable entry point for newcomers to the faith and the church will become increasingly important.
- Reframing from a centralized approach to Christian education to a decentralized approach to spiritual formation is a challenge we face.
- Integrating faith formation and daily life is a challenge before us.
- We must assess objectively whether we are building barriers or bridges to our learners and seekers.

Serving in the Trenches and Not Just in Church Programs

Deacons have been serving Christ and the Church since the days of the early church. Strategies and methodologies have changed throughout church history. Different needs, cultures and communication abilities are once again forcing us to rethink our definitions of deacon ministry, service and success in ministry. We can no longer ignore the realities of our unchurched culture:

- Researchers of the unchurched culture inform us that about 60–70 percent of our population are considered unchurched. George Barna's research indicates that at least one-third of all adults are unchurched in the USA.[7] These have little or no understanding or appreciation of those church words, hymns, and religious rituals we have been and are nurtured by.

- Those Christ calls the churches to reach, no longer flock to our church programs or services. We are challenged an mandated to "Go into all the world . . . . into the fields that are white unto harvest."
- The secularization of our society (and in many cases our churches) presents today's church with issues, problems and areas of brokenness we've rarely known or seen before. We are now being called to train for and serve in the trenches — the tough places of our culture and society, if the lost are to be won, the broken are to be restored and the hopeless are to find hope (Isa 61, Matt 5). Our children are attending schools filled with violence, cruelty, and flashes of family dysfunction among their classmates, teachers, and administrators.

We are being called to follow Christ in servanthood. Isaiah reminds us "that those who wait upon the Lord will renew their strength. They will soar upon wings like eagles, they will run and not grow weary, they will walk and not be faint" (Isa 40:31). As we learn lessons of servanthood let me remind us that the "wait" Isaiah is talking about is not lingering in dormancy, rather he is suggesting we "serve the Lord like a waiter in a restaurant." He calls us to active servanthood, not a passive searching or spectatorship.

Let's quickly review some of Christ's model of servanthood found in scripture:

- Jesus and the woman at the well
- Jesus offering healing to the blind beggar at the pool outside the temple
- Jesus offering healing to the paralytic dropped before him by his friends
- Jesus reaching out to the woman with the issue of blood
- Jesus taking care of the widows, the children and the needy

Luke 10 is often referred to as a manual for ministry and reminds us of the servanthood character of ministry; inconvenience, toughness and loneliness.

Bill Easum, author of *Growing Spiritual Redwoods* and *Sacred Cows Make Good Hamburgers,* helps us understand a little clearer some of the shifts in our understanding and practice of servanthood in the twenty-first century church. Let's review quickly some of these shifts:

Declining Congregation *Members are:*	*Thriving Congregation* *Participants are:*
Committed to the church	Committed to Christ
Managing committees	Deploying Missions
Holding offices	Doing hands-on ministries
Making decisions	Making disciples
Trained for membership	On a life long quest for quality
Serving the church	Serving in the world
Preoccupied with raising money	Preoccupied with rescuing people
Doing church work	Finding personal fulfillment
Retiring from church work	Sensitizing themselves to community
Surveying internal needs	Eager for everyone to know God
Loyal to each other	Drawn to the unchurched
Building on faith information	Building faith on experience with Christ
Perpetuating a heritage	Visioning a future

From Bill Easum, *Growing Spiritual Redwoods* (Nashville: Abingdon Press, 2000), 3-4.

Hints for training and serving in the trenches:

• Remember: Move toward your fears. "Perfect love casts out all fear." We are now called to wrestle with our fears and our prejudice about the divorced, those from broken homes and blended families, persons with AIDS and their caregivers, persons with different values, lifestyles, and cultural diversities.

• You're called to be a spiritual role model for ministry before your congregation. Where will your congregation end up by following your personal example? Of servanthood? Of ministry? Giving? Going?

• Be intentional about developing your spiritual walk. You can't give what you don't have and you can't talk people to where you have never been.

• Keep one foot in the church, but the other in the world. Unless we know about the realities of the world we're in we cannot design effective ministries. We'll continue to be found guilty of only designing churches and programs for church people and not for reaching or ministering to the lost outside the church.

• Ask at every meeting, "What are the realities of the world I encounter daily and what does God want me/us to do about the needs and realities we see?"

• Nominate and elect spiritually minded, servant-hearted people to serve as deacons for the twenty-first century church. We must have servants who have a strong relationship with Christ and a burden and compassion for upgrading the church and reaching the unchurched for Christ.

Serving and training in the trenches is more than balancing budgets, taking care of the building and grounds and monitoring personnel and business affairs of the church. It is equipping ourselves to walk with the dying, persons who are unemployed, persons suffering from substance, physical or sexual abuse or those touched by violence or other social ills. It is learning to practice the presence of Christ to those who struggle with addictions, those struggling with caring for aging parents, or those working with issues related to living out their faith in the workplace, or whether they will embrace euthanasia, genetic engineering or thoughts or gestures of suicide. The challenges of the new century are certain to be great. Will you follow Christ there? Or will you stay in the comfort of your pews or unchallenged beliefs of your comfortable past?

Learning to serve in the trenches is a basic characteristic of those leaders who can lead a congregation to move beyond its comfort zone of maintenance and self care to a congregation that is on mission. A congregation will never move beyond its spiritual leadership. To transition a congregation you will need visionary, bold models of

---

Reframing Hints To Ponder

• The unchurched culture brings with it many new challenges to churches and church leaders.

• Churches need to revisit their call to servant hood in our broken world.

• There are major differences in the focus of congregations on the decline and those thriving congregations.

servanthood to lead the church to be the church inside and outside the walls.

Will Life Coaches Parallel Sunday School Teachers?

While I am keenly aware of the excellent faith development research of persons like Horace Bushnell, James Fowler, John Westerhoff, James Dystra, Bruce Powers, Robert Wurthnow, Linda Vogel, and Kenneth Stokes, I think the secular age and a high spiritual thirst in our land pushes us to look at discipleship through a different lens than traditional "faith formation theorists." In light of the increasing interest in spiritual formation of leaders in an increasingly secular world, what avenues might not only exist but could be fertile and available ground for Christian education and discipleship? Seems to me that the coaching network, business and relationships might be the new avenues emerging for a church to facilitate spiritual formation. Could a church appoint, train, and resource Christian coaches who would function on a parallel track to elected Sunday school or church program leaders? The curricula of the Christian life coach could include:

- Identifying those searchers or seekers in their circle of influence;
- Building bridges to healthy relationships;
- Coaching them in unfreezing old unwanted habits, attitudes, behaviors; and
- Coaching them in refreezing into habits, attitudes, behaviors and skills that would be more life-giving and liberating.

Identifying Searchers or Seekers

Life coaches would be those persons who are gifted as teachers, counselors, or encouragers and have a strong discernment about persons who might be seekers or searchers. They would enjoy helping persons move forward in life, in professional skills, relational skills, family skills, or mending from grief or dysfunction in their history. Helping persons develop or refine such life skills and/or unlock them from the dysfunction or grief of their past can propel them into a more effective and meaningful future, but also help them find spiritual grounding and community in the journey. Such a calling would find a new avenue for expression through life coaching. It seems to me that such might be the emergence of a parallel track for persons who for whatever reason aren't ready for or desirous of participating in the traditional Sunday school or discipling functions of the church.

Life coaches would find support, resourcing, prayer, nurture, and equipping from their local church. These coaches would then begin to pray for and be attentive to those persons God places in their path that are seekers or searchers. Who are those people in your circle of influence? Once you connect to one or two persons and walk with them as a life coach they will refer others to you — it's really like a web. When you help one they bring two others for similar help. "Could this be a new outreach strategy?" might be the response of some. Certainly that might be the case, but it should not be the primary motivation. The primary motivation for being a life coach is to help persons move forward. Paul talks about those who are "gold in the making." Many are in the heated furnace of life trials and struggles and can't find a place in the traditional church. They might respond very well to one who comes alongside of them for an extended period of time and becomes a guide, and sometimes a midwife for that which God is trying to bring forth.

Building Bridges not Barriers as a Coach

In the unchurched, secular culture in which we minister in the twenty-first century, building relationships is critically important. The Christian community and churchpersons are having to earn the right to be heard. We are having to earn the respect, trust, and confidence of those outside our faith and outside our church walls. We do this by being involved in their world in healthy ways. Finding those places that God can use us in their life to help them find and take the next step toward wholeness and health. Let's review some of the bridge builders from my own coaching journey:

• We have to understand that when relating to and earning the respect of those in the unchurched world we will encounter value systems, behaviors, attitudes and lifestyles we might not agree with or endorse. However, it is vitally important, in earning respect not to judge them, but to love them, to walk with them and to help them experience the unconditional love of God through you. Such is a critical step in building bridges. Judging and hostility only build more barriers between "us" and "them."

• Learning to be comfortable with and clear with their communication style and language. I've learned the hard way, on many occasions, that I'm much more comfortable talking with people who share my "church language." Unchurched people are not comfortable with it. We must meet them where they are. I'm not asking that we adopt their language necessarily; I am asking that we not let their language be a barrier to our coaching. I've discovered on more than one occasion that an unchurched person uses different words to talk about their spiritual journey than I would — but that doesn't necessarily mean that spiritual experience is inauthentic. Meeting them where they are, as Jesus did in his ministry, is a bridge builder. Getting them to change to our comfort zone is a barrier builder.

• Build a bridge to them through daily prayer and consistent dialogue opportunities. Listening to them, caring for them and being a channel of celebration and growth for them.

Coaching: Unfreezing The Old

Life coaching is based in Paul's admonition that "in Christ all things become new" and that the "old passes away." The coaching relationship finds various manifestations and challenges. "Coaching" terminology itself is a term accepted by the secular culture, whereas many of the coaching skills are similar to, if not parallel with biblically-based discipling skills.

As the coaching relationship matures that is being bathed in prayer, discernment and reflection often trust is built in life areas needing work. It begins to become clear either to the coach or to person being coached or both that the issues are deeper and broader than first imagined. In some cases the attitudes, habits, behaviors, or false belief systems need to be "thawed out." That is they have been part of their life for so long that the person typically doesn't even know another way is out there. So unfreezing the old comes as you begin to mirror reality for them, acknowledge discrepancies and point them to other ways of coping or responding to a given situation. Reframing of life and developing new life skills are at the root of good life coaching in a secular culture.

Coaching: Refreezing The New

In a secular culture, one of the challenges we face is not only unfreezing the old attitudes, or behaviors but also finding ways to introduce those issues of life transformation. Transformation through spiritual empowerment is the goal, but the challenge is to find ways and the means that the unchurched, secular minded person can relate to and become engaged with to build momentum in their spiritual growth. Coaching someone toward progress, success, deeper self-awareness, and effectiveness are usually life goals worthy of serious attention.

Let me illustrate. Bo, a corporate businessman, a self-proclaimed agnostic, was in my doctoral group several years ago. He was working on a project on how to help his business become more "customer-friendly, customer-oriented, and service-minded." Since I was the only minister he had ever known personally and because he was curious about me and the Bible's teachings, he inquired, "Is there anything in your discipline that might help me in my project?"

From this, Bo and I developed an online and phone relationship. I pointed him to the management principles found in the book of Nehemiah. Shared the principles with him — he validated their business savvy and then I gave him the Biblical references. We read and critiqued together *Hand Me Another Brick* by Charles Swindoll, which consists of sermons from this biblical text and focuses on servanthood. I was praying for Bo, his family, and his business and also that God would continue to make me sensitive to "teachable moments" and "divine appointments" in my relationship with Bo. Things continued to progress. Bo's questions grew more frequent and his interest and curiosity in biblical and management principles continued. To make a long story short, I was able to witness Bo unfreezing some of his past beliefs about clergy, scripture, and some management principles and embracing and owning new beliefs and attitudes. The next thing I knew he was teaching these principles, from Nehemiah, to his management team. Over a three year period God did an amazing work in Bo, his business, and in me. I learned much about discerning God's movement in life, learning to be attentive to the Holy Spirit and leadership in others, and learning to find language that communicated spiritual truths without religious baggage or barriers.

Reframing life and providing consistent care, nurture and guidance assist persons in refreezing a new lifestyle, priorities, and beliefs. Coaching develops character, life skills, spiritual pathways and the embracing of new life transforming truths. What great joy, fulfillment and hope occurs when the unfreezing and refreezing are complete.

Randy, the young professional I've previously mentioned, said to me just recently that he has been "so amazed, so grateful and feels so graced" because of all the internal changes that have occurred that are now allowing him to develop personally, professionally and relationally. He's found a new life and new energy since he's been released from addictive patterns, dysfunctional behaviors, false beliefs and has aligned his internal world with his external world. He's found forgiveness for himself, for his parents, and new hope for his future. He's worked very hard, but as he says, "the work has been worth it!"

Life coaching can be a significant means of spiritual transformation, a way of introducing the Good News and growing people toward

Reframing Hints To Ponder

- The coaching network, business and social relationships might be the new avenues emerging for a church to facilitate spiritual formation.
- Life coaches would enjoy helping persons move forward in life, in professional skills, relational skills, family skills or mending from grief or dysfunction in their history.
- Many are in the heated furnace of life trials and struggles and can not find a place in many traditional churches.
- In an unchurched culture, building relationships is critically important.
- The Christian community and churches are having to earn the right to be heard.
- We need to discover and work the bridge builders for effective ministry.
- Reframing of life and developing new life skills are at the root of good life coaching in a secular culture.

wholeness, holiness and maturity. Coaching serves as a vital and strategic means of spiritual formation in a secular age.

Utilizing Spiritual Formation Engineers and Life Transformation Teams

Spiritual Formation Engineers

Can we create effective learning loops during the week and between various people and media sources to facilitate spiritual formation? How can we create learning portals via the internet that will utilize life experiences, throughout the week, to facilitate spiritual formation? Could this venue been effective as outreach or a catalyst for an energizing gathering on Sundays? A major research project "Wired Churches, Wired Temples: Taking Congregations and Missions in to Cyberspace" (www.pewinternet.org) has uncovered that 21 percent of Internet users (about 19 to 20 million people) have used Internet to seek spiritual and religious information. Also, 83 percent of respondents noted that their websites had helped congregational life "some" or a "great deal" and 81 percent agree that at some level email has helped improve the spiritual life of the congregation.[11]

Is there a way to engage target groups with sermons, the Christian calendar, and spiritual formation via the multiplicity of media sources throughout the week as an introduction to the content and relationships or as a follow up to what was experienced while church was "in session"? (See resource list at the end of this chapter.) Connecting the "gathered church experience" to the "scattered church experience" is a missing link that we need to address and media sources can facilitate *if* we are willing to adapt and rethink the way we do Christian education. (See my *The Gathered and Scattered Church* for additional information.)

Could we build "Bible study classes," "discipleship groups," "mission groups," or "ministry teams" online? Virtual classes/groups might birth new cyber-communities and learning portals that could literally benefit not only from peer learning, coaching and mentoring relationships, but also begin to facilitate multicultural and multi-ethnic dialogues as well. E-learning (electronic learning) seems to be the wave of the future. Increasing numbers of persons of all age groups, all ethnic groups and language groups are going online.

The internet is literally changing the way the world does training, learning, service, information, sales, auctions, dating, investing, and communication. Such a rapid shift in is challenging all institutions in our world. The church seems to think she doesn't have to pay attention to this trend that's just for the secular business community. *I, for one, believe if the church doesn't pay serious and immediate attention to e-learning we will take another giant step toward irrelevancy in the minds of our constituency.* How then can the congregation become a "learning organization" so as to benefit from the learnings of all those in attendance and in our communities so we can strategize to accelerate and update the pace of learning and spiritual formation?

Is there a way to customize and regionalize curricula by utilizing local programming (radio, TV, newspaper, and local events, etc.) as a piece of the learning portal for this weeks/months Bible study, spiritual formation class, mission experience, or ministry opportunity? Could this be a new role for diocese, associations, or state conventions? What if every diocese, state convention or association had a "spiritual formation designer or team" on their staff to help facilitate this learning loop/objective? What if literature and learning tools/resources were emailed or faxed to teachers and or churches from this office on a week to week or month to month basis instead of from a national publishing house? Might this increase interest, motivation, accountability and relevancy? Seems that we might need a Spiritual Formation Engineer Team and Life Transformation Teams rather than Sunday School Councils, Women's Missionary Union, or Baptist Men. That is not to say we don't need the traditional groupings, it is to say we need to rethink their focus and the way we engineer their curricula. Are we trying to perpetuate organizations to serve the church or design experiences to transform the people? Consider . . .

What would a Spiritual Formation Engineer do?

• Create a research and design team among church and community leaders to help discover appropriate experiences and information for regionalized curricula.

- Work with research and design team to customize information and experiences to appropriate phases of the spiritual journey, biblical narratives, and various learning portals or opportunities.
- Work with church and community leaders to identify and appropriately resource common life experiences, rites of passage and life stages.
- Discover the most appropriate venue for learning for each of these people groups/target groups and customize Bible-focused and experiential curricula to facilitate spiritual formation of the learners.
- Celebrate the learnings and create opportunities for networking and coaching each group involved in the learning loops.

Frequently the voiced fears to this approach is that such interfacing with media, internet or life experience takes us away from study of the Bible or that it takes us away from traditional church structures. My experience has been quite the contrary. Utilizing these approaches has created forums and teachable moments to intersect with biblical narratives and has created comfortable nonthreatening entry points for persons on a spiritual journey. Often persons initially reached or ministered to in these learning portals do not find their way into traditional structures quickly, but without these venues they often are not cultivated or reached at all.

For instance ,what would happen if you negotiated with a local movie theater to purchase an advertisement they would show prior to a movie with a spiritual theme inviting viewers of the movie to stay afterward or to meet you in a local coffee shop for "movie dialogue"? I've tried this and those who viewed *The Green Mile* and felt that "holy hush" at the conclusion of the movie met me for coffee and dialogue. The group has met for several times to pursue truth and understanding. Community is building among some of us that continue to meet. I can't wait to see what happens as God continues to work through our relationships which were initiated by a secular film with a spiritual message.

Life Transformation Teams

If we are in the business of "being not conformed to this world, but being transformed by the renewing of your heart and mind" maybe we need to consider the focus a Life Transformation Team could bring. The primary focus of this team will be to seek out, acknowledge and utilize life passages, experiences and rites of passage as teaching places to help reframe life and focus such experiences in light of the Good News.

What might a Life Transformation Team do?

• Identify the primary rites of passage of persons in the church and community.
• Seek out ways to validate and transform these life experiences into healthy spiritual transformation experiences.
• Create ways to network persons in each life experience for an ongoing support and transformation ministry.
• Connect persons involved in these identified rites of passages and life experiences to each other, to others in the community of like experiences and ultimately to Christ and the Church.
• Seek out resources (media, print, internet, organizations, and persons) that can facilitate the process of spiritual transformation.
• Create a prayer ministry of support for each segment of this process and each person involved as team member and participant.
• Provide reframing opportunities designed to refocus or focus on the Good News which will nurture and inform new growth through life experiences.

For instance, the Life Transformation Team might identify those couples with an empty nest, where children have left for college or marriage relationships. This team could connect these couples determine the health of their marriage relationship and faith and help them discern their calling and gifts. From this they might reframe this life stage with the birthing of a ministry. The ministry might be that they become a mentoring marriage for newlyweds, or maybe they provide the empty bedroom in their home to a needy person — maybe a mother that is pregnant out of wedlock. They would then study and pray with other couples and seek to find their story in His Story. The church would validate, support and encourage them in this new life stage. These couples would then be involved in meaningful Bible study, prayer, mission, ministry, and *koinonia* with persons of like heart and mind. This is a step toward maximizing our calling, our time, our gifts and the integrating of our Christian education curricula and experience. The essence of curricula seems to be emerging more from the movements of God in one's life and world than from the publishing houses or institutional programs of an institutional church.

Reframing Hints To Ponder

- In an age where customer service is the mantra the church seems to be clinging to the same services we've provided for decades.
- Most of our leaders have been in the same system of doing church that we can't begin to imagine doing church any other way.
- I think we need to re-read the Book of the Acts of the Apostles.
- This reformation is challenging not doctrine but the very medium through which the message of Christianity is articulated.
- Can we create effective learning loops during the week and between various people and media sources to facilitate spiritual formation in a busy world?
- Connecting the "gathered church experience" to the "scattered church experience" is a missing link that we need to address and media sources can facilitate if we are willing to adapt and rethink the way we do Christian education.
- If the church doesn't pay attention to e-learning we will take another giant step toward irrelevancy in the minds of our constituency.
- Providing reframing opportunities designed to refocus or focus on the Good News which will nurture and inform new growth through life experiences.
- The essence of curricula seems to be emerging more from the movements of God in one's life and world than from publishing houses or institutional programs of an institutional church.

Rediscovering the Depths of the New Birth: Paying Attention to Rites of Passage

"God so loved the world that He gave . . . " (John 3:16)
"While we were yet sinners Christ died for us . . . " (Rom 5:8)
"Except you be born again you can not enter the Kingdom of Heaven."
(John 3:3, 5)

These are representative of verses I memorized early in my Christian journey. I heard about the new birth in my childhood years and came to understand from my Sunday School teachers and parents that there was something wrong and Jesus could make it better. I came to understand that Jesus loved me very much, so much so that whenever I did do things wrong, He would forgive me. Now it wasn't until my teenage years that I walked down the aisle to accept Christ as my savior. Some would say that was my new birth. In acutality, I think that walk gave a public voice to a rebirth that had been going on in me for many years and because of many experiences. When I talk of conversion I talk of many mini-conversions. Jesus died to save me in the past, but God is saving me now, and will continue to save me in the future. The God I serve is into growth, into helping me and us change into God's likeness throughout life. God calls for us to give back each aspect and avenue of our lives daily. God even challenges us "to pick up our cross daily." Part of that cross for me is deciding to give God those challenges and opportunities of my daily life so I can be taught through them (See Appendix B).

While all of these truths are still true in a secular culture, the way we experience and lead people to understand and embrace them are likely to be different and often more challenging for those of us who were raised in a church culture and were familiar with biblical language. How does a secular minded, nonchurch person come to experience and embrace spiritual conversion(s)? How do they learn to pay attention to the "eurekas" of their life? How do they learn that God loves them, that an extraordinary thing was done for them because of that love, and that a promise of new life has been offered to them if they choose to follow Christ?

Bill Easum helps the church leader understand the postmodern mindset and the challenges that brings to our traditional church. He declares:

> The modern world took a cognitive approach to discipleship, beginning with belief, moving to belonging and resulting in behaving. Today's experiential culture requires just the opposite. Discipleship moves from changing one's behavior, to becoming part of a community of friends, to belief in the God seen in those new friends' lives. The day of walking the aisle for Jesus is disappearing in the Western world.[8]

He further suggests, "the Emmaus experience in Luke 24 gives us a better way of describing conversion today." He offers the following implications from the shift from "being saved" to "being transformed."

• Primarily, in the Western world, conversion takes longer — perhaps two to three years and requires more people along the way.
• We must view evangelism as a systematic process rather than a program — evangelism becomes the mission of everyone not just a committee.
• Instead of evangelism as a mostly "one-to-one" experience, it seems to be moving more toward a group process. Paul's formula in 1 Corinthians 3:6 seems to offer good guidance for this century.
• In "contextual evangelism" non-Christians respond better to groups or individuals with the same life experiences they have had (i.e., alcoholic to recovering alcoholic, etc.)
• Affirmation evangelism is essential in this long-term process. Christian's need to learn to acknowledge God's presence and work in the lives of those around them.
• A number of evangelistic alliances are forming today that have nothing to do with denominations but are designed to reach this postmodern world for Christ.[9]

Stanley Grenz is another pioneer in helping us understand the postmodern mindset and world. In an article entitled, "The Quest for a Communal Spirituality in the Postmodern World," he suggests, "in one sense the current interest in spirituality is the contemporary, postmodern embodiment of the age-old human search for personal identity. The chaos of identity marks the contemporary spiritual quest." Grenz's research seems to suggest that the spiritual quest of the postmodern is in their relationships with each other rather than finding a home with God. Therefore, how do we encourage a connection with others and ultimately with God?[10]

I've grappled with these and many other questions over the last 15 years of my journey as I've opened myself to learning to relate to and communicate effectively with those who are spiritually thirsty but unchurched. I think if we paid more attention to the rites of passage of life's common experiences, we could not only help others understand the changes of life, but help them find guidance and wholeness in making those changes. Building community among those making common changes tends to help the unchurched find and experience a loving, redemptive community. They come to learn trust of others that ultimately can be transferred to God.

Let me illustrate. I met with Suzanne, a neighbor and an international law attorney for a major industry, at our community mailboxes one day. I really didn't know Suzanne; we had only met one or two other times. I noted that it appeared she had been crying. I remarked with some concern and caution, "Looks like you've had a tough day."

She looked at me with eyes filled with hurt and grief and said, "I've just heard from my brother in Pittsburgh that my mother died this morning and I have no idea who we will get to bury her. We've never been to church, I've never even been to a funeral before." I expressed my sympathy to her and indicated if there was any way I could help her I would be glad to do so. I offered to take her to the airport and to make some calls for her. After a moment of silence she looked at me and asked, "Do you know anyone that could bury my mother?"

I then shared with her that I was a minister and that if she desired I would be willing to do the funeral service or see if I could find someone in the Pittsburgh area. It was if a heavy burdened were suddenly lifted from her. She hugged my neck and said "Oh, that would be so helpful if you could help us with her funeral." To make a long story short, I flew with her to Pittsburgh, did her mother's funeral, and spent hours listening to her family and trying to facilitate the beginning of their grief work. Over the next months Suzanne and I talked frequently and I watched her searching heart find refuge in the God of love that I talked about at her Mom's funeral. She then became part of a group of unchurched persons that I put together and met with consistently in their search for truth and wholeness.

It was the availability, the willingness to listen without judgment to her heartaches and questions about life and death, and my invitation to her to continue that dialogue in a comfortable nonthreatening environment that invited her to continue to grow in her spiritual journey. After about a year and half I was privileged to lead Suzanne to Christ. She too experienced many mini-conversions before she made her faith commitment public. She realized God loved her, that God had a plan for her life and was working it out over time because of a care for her. She came to release some of the grief and even anger over her Mom's death and to create a bond of trust with other persons on a similar journey.

Another example of new birth came from my relationship with a lady in her 70's who was lonely, isolated from family and friends, and harboring much anger toward her family and God because of a string of tragedies that she had lived through over the last 40 years. I encountered her at a bookstore — she loved to read. We engaged in dialogue about gardening, ended up sharing a cup of coffee and the relationship began. She was Methodist, even went to church occasionally, but really "went out of obligation and guilt." She really wanted to experience God, but was "having trouble believing or finding God in this world filled with injustice, evil, and cruelty." Verna and I decided to keep talking. I walked with her through much heartache, pain, deep questions probing her pain and her theology over several years. She introduced me to family as "one who is helping me find God." She often said she wished her church had a place and people to help her out of her pit of despair. She felt they didn't care about anything but her presence at their services and her tithe. I felt blessed to be able to watch God do several redemptive acts in her life and family as well as give her the reassurance she desired and needed of God's presence and care. She died several years ago and I was asked by her family to do the funeral. I was privileged and honored by their invitation.

The point here is that the journey of spiritual formation in a secular age often begins by focusing on people and not programs or even their conversion. It also seems that acknowledging the rites of passage that persons face and encounter as teachable moments and divine appointments may be the very open door to spiritual formation the church longs to find. I hope that we would begin to pay closer attention to the rites of passage and discover ways to walk with persons, to facilitate the grace, forgiveness and presence of God in their midst during those times. Simply walking with them and learning to listen to them so they will talk and discover the great release and forgiveness that is available, offers the greatest track and opportunity for spiritual formation we could ever have. In a secular culture it's not so important to "teach the Word" in classes as it is to "incarnate the Word" through the lives and relationships we encounter. These encounters then earn us the right to be heard so when we teach, we can be heard and trusted. It might be that we need to learn to "be" more than "do."

Reframing Hints To Ponder

- How does a secular minded, non-churched person come to experience and embrace spiritual conversion?
- Discipleship moves from changing one's behavior, to becoming part of a community of friends, to belief in God seen in those new friends' lives.
- The day of walking the aisle for Jesus is disappearing in the Western world.
- How do we encourage connecting with each other and ultimately with God?
- Paying more attention to life's passages might be a new avenue for spiritual formation.
- Spiritual formation in a secular age often begins with focusing on people and not programs or even their conversion.

Think about the life events and experiences that provide avenues for "rites of passage" and opportunities for ministry to those persons you encounter on a regular basis? What is the Spirit leading you to be and do to incarnate His love, grace, mercy, hope, forgiveness and redemption in those life situations?

Reframing for Spiritual Formation in a Secular Culture

Reframing *for* spiritual formation rather than reframing Christian education is the challenge we face. Such acknowledges that we are no longer in a Christian or church culture; that we are living in the midst of great pluralism and diversity; that coming to Christ and experiencing sanctification begins by meeting people where they are and moving them step by step toward greater understanding of and practice of their walk with God. It focuses us on growing people in faith — forming their spiritual foundations and relationships. If we were to try to reframe Christian education we would likely try different didactic model shifts — curricula, teaching methodology, teacher training, room arrangements, use of different visual aids, etc. The reframing of spiritual formation follows more of the Spiritual Formation Model, and the Celtic Model — which focuses on intentional reframing of relationships, framework of dialogues and seeking out and maximizing teachable moments and divine appointments. The Engel Scale helps provide a functional gauge for such a process; The Spiritual Formation Guide provides help in reading and reframing the story of one's life, the Distinctives of Disciplemaking Phases, provides a biblical framework based on the ministry of Christ. Another way of looking at the difference between reframing Christian education and reframing spiritual formation might be clarified with the following chart:

Reframing Spiritual Formation		Reframing Christian Education
Focus on people	not just	institutional programs
Focusing on inner development	not just	outward behavioral life responses
Soul craft focus	not just	institutional focus

As I've struggled with the need for such reframing I have found the following charting strategy to be a helpful guideline and framework for intentional prayer, planning, study, reflection, evaluation, and relationship building.

A Strategy for Prayer, Planning, and Relationship Building

This strategy is built around four significant phases of disciplemaking. Different people use different words to work with these disciplemaking concepts. I'm choosing to build this grid around *attract, assimilate, disciple, deploy.* It is important in our planning to grow people in Christ to remember that people enter our spiritual formation processes at different times and at different places in their spiritual journey. Therefore, note that in the chart "Reframing for Spiritual Formation" in Appendix C, we begin with those we are trying to *attract.* Next we begin with those we have already attracted and have some relationship with. Now, we are trying to effectively *assimilate* those we have attracted. Then there may be those we have attracted and begun to assimilate, but are now needed to guide their *discipleship.*

In **Section 1** of the chart we begin by identifying some of the key people groups you are trying to *attract.* This would be persons you are aware of that are in your community, but are unchurched. It might include assessing who are the persons that your congregational members are already aware of, burdened by and/or connected to. List those groups (i.e., nonbelievers married to believers).

In **Section 2** we ask what are some comfortable nonthreatening events/experiences (comfortable and non-threatening to those we are trying to reach not those of us already involved) that might attract these persons. How do you identify and work within a "Come and See" experience/event? Most of our traditional outreach strategies or Christian education classes are very threatening or unfamiliar for the unchurched. How do we meet them on their turf, so they may be more comfortable so we can build bridges of relationships. Now let me quick to say — frequently if they are more comfortable, we churchpersons are uncomfortable. This is the sacrifice we may have to make to reach them. I'm confident Christ didn't always find great "personal comfort" in some of the places he found himself — at least they were probably not his personal preference for use of His time and energies. For instance, the many events/experiences he spent with

120

sinners rather than in the temple or in personal leisure. Or all those fishing expeditions or breakfasts on the sea shore.

In **Section 3** take this group you've attracted to the next step by asking how can we *assimilate* them. How can we work with them and work with our church persons to build a bridge of understanding and belonging? How can we help them genuinely feel they belong, they are wanted, that we really do want to unconditionally accept them and that we really do receive them "just as they are" (we sing many verses of "Just As I Am" — now we're having to live it out.) Next brainstorm, pray and strategize with others seeking to assimilate this group the how, when, who and where and why of this aspect of ministry.

In **Section 4**, as they begin to feel assimilated and build relationships of trust and authenticity with us, ask "how do we *disciple* them?" That is, how do we meet people where they are in their spiritual journey and guide them in taking their next steps toward greater understanding of truth and decided adjustments in attitudes, behaviors and acts of justice. See, we are working with a group from one phase to another in their own spiritual formation. The agenda is really built around God's movement in their life rather than our institutional goals or our personal preferences. How do we find and discern God's movement in their lives? How do we find God at work and join Him there? How can we facilitate and acknowledge God's work in their lives in ways they can hear and appreciate? How can we

Reframing Hints To Ponder

- Reframing for spiritual formation is the challenge we face rather than reframing Christian education.
- It focuses on growing people in faith.
- Built on the discipling model of Christ — come and see, come and follow me, come and be with me and come and abide in me.
- Spiritual formation is built upon learning to attract, assimilate, disciple, and deploy believers and non-believers.
- Spiritual formation must take life passages seriously and the art of spiritual direction and theological reflection on life experiences.
- Spiritual formation is a personal and a community experience.

begin to do some theological reflection on their life experiences in ways they can grasp?

In **Section 5**, begin to ask and pray about *deploying* them. How can a mentoring relationship be created to help them explore ministry possibilities? How can hurts, healings of heart, mind and family be used by God as avenues of witness and ministry?

Such a format simply helps us begin with people, with people's search for truth, and barriers they have to finding God rather than our agendas, programs, and curricula. It's the essence of incarnational theology. God came in the flesh and dwelt among us. How do you find and experience God in the midst of this world of diverse pain, struggle, joy, celebration and challenge? A blank chart is included in Appendix D for your use.

Team-Based Ministry Builds Community

Since spiritual formation is not only an individual but a community experience, team ministry has real possibilities in a person's spiritual journey. In the secular age we live in relationships are critically important. Many who are spiritually thirsty and searching are in need of relationships where trust, healing, hope, forgiveness, negotiation, redemption and love can be experienced. The experiences become a critical part of one's spiritual formation. Without such relationships many are likely not to move forward in their search. This and many other issues are why teams are increasingly important.

In the church culture committees were of vital importance in maintaining the church. Today the shift to teams creates just the forums needed for spiritual growth that is authentic, active and based in a faith community. Teams can be a nonthreatening and comfortable entry point for persons who may not be ready to enter a church service or a church-based program, but they can contribute their strengths to a team.

Committees are usually forever, without a clear focus or leader, while teams are short-term, focused, and often shared leadership facilitated toward a goal. Teams are great places for building community spirit, motivation and exercising gifts of many persons who will help for a short-term project that fuels their passion. Team-based ministry is an answer to many of the leadership crises and assimilation challenges churches are facing these days. Consider some of the common leadership and assimilation dilemmas:

• Declining interest in serving as a deacon and growing needs of pastoral care of the congregation and community
• Leadership burnout because of few leaders holding multiple responsibilities
• Growing ministries/programs without an increasing leadership base
• Members joining, but not connecting to the faith or the congregation
• Converts being birthed into the Kingdom, but not nurtured in the faith
• Spiritually thirsty persons searching for life's answers and not enough disciplemakers or disciplemaking structures in place
• Persons attending but not joining
• Persons joining but not getting involved

Team-based ministry is not just a name change, it's a philosophical shift in thinking and activity!

Gary McIntosh helps us see the value of teams and puts them in historical and practical perspective.

THEN	NOW
More structure-driven	More mission-driven
People served more out of duty & obligation	Serving out of their passion and gifting
More informational	More relational
More leader dependent	Greater shared responsibility for the team
More top-down authority & information shared by the leader	Team is getting input and information for everyone
Leader driven	Facilitator led
Power & control were the issue	Empowerment of team is issue
Team focused on a task or relationship	Team focused on task & relationship
Leadership was assigned or transferred	Leadership emerges from the team[11]

Instead of assigning all pastoral care giving to the ministerial staff and/or the deacons, broaden the scope of your ministry and structures to include teams of those many gifted persons who have a calling and passion to care for specific people groups. The diverse and growing emotional, physical, spiritual and relational needs of our church population, not to mention our communities, is much more than a few can handle or even equip themselves for. That is why many churches are exploring a broader organization. For instance some are connecting deacon ministry, Sunday School group/care leaders, and ministry teams. Others are setting up a laypastoring ministry where laypersons and clergy work together to meet pastoral care needs. Still others develop and utilize support groups as the hub of their pastoral care ministries.

Let me make a couple of suggestions where teams can serve as comfortable non-threatening entry points and a vital part of spiritual formation:

• Handbell Choirs
• Vocal Ensembles
• Sports/recreation teams
• Habitat for Humanity teams
• Mission Trip Teams
• Orchestra or praise bands

Someone is likely to remark, "How can nonbelievers or non church members be part of these various groups — these groups lead in worship, or are on mission to share the story?" Why can't these groups/teams begin to function as a small discipleship group, build trust and community while doing the tasks at hand and nurture the non-believer, while that non-believer or non church member, contributes something he/she is good at and thus has a comfortable non-threatening entry point into our community of faith? This is a shift that is difficult for many church culture leaders, but is a critical shift for churches who are seeking to create forums for the spiritual formation of those who are searching for truth in our unchurched/secular culture.

We can use teams to facilitate spiritual formation. Being more focused and intentional that the group has a discipling function in the body of Christ as well as a task function that serves as the comfortable entry point. Delegating responsibility and handing off tasks that persons are capable of doing or contributing to becomes a piece of building trust, relationships and community.

Delegation — Key to Leadership

Leaders with high influence understand delegation. They don't always do it, but they do understand the concept and seek some competence in this arena. It's not complicated, but it does require some intentional actions on the part of the leader in order to be effective. Delegation is particularly challenging with volunteers.

Alister Emerson, from Christchurch, New Zealand, suggests four sharp questions for leaders as they delegate to volunteers:

• *What have you done since our last check-in?* Periodic reports keep the project moving. This helps workers who get bogged down see what is slowing progress.

• *In the process of doing your task, what did you run into, both positive and negative?*
Here you gain insight into the person's attitude about the project. Leaders often focus on the negative because problems demand attention. This question lifts workers above the hard slog and gives reason to celebrate.

• *What did you do about what you ran into, both positive and negative?* This reveals whether the volunteer is really suited for the job. And this is the most valuable teaching opportunity. Here you can congratulate them for finding solutions, offer suggestions for alternate approaches, and assess their abilities to give and take direction.

• *What are you going to do next?* This question keeps the volunteer on task, affirms the person's responsibility for developing the project and moving it along. If they are unsure, you can suggest future actions.[12]

Reframing Hints To Ponder

- Teams can be an effective instrument of spiritual formation.
- Team-based ministry is an answer to many of the leadership and pastoral care crises and assimilation challenges churches are facing these days.
- Leaders with high influence understand delegation.

These illustrations are only indicative of the many team ministries that can be formed to help spread the leadership base, develop new leaders, energize leaders by allowing them opportunity to work from their gifts and passions. At the end of this chapter is a list of resources to help with the many aspects of team-based ministry.

Notes

[1] See Bill Hull's *Revival That Reforms* and *Jesus Christ the Disciplemaker* (New Jersey: Revell Press, 1999) and F. F. Bruce's *The Training of the Twelve* (New Jersey: Revell Press, 1999) for more information on the disciplemaking ministry of Jesus.

[2] John Shea, *The Spirit Master* (Philadelphia: Thomas Moore Press, 1987), 132-35.

[3] Ibid., 132-35.

[4] C. Ellis Nelson, *How Faith Matures* (Louisville: Westminster John Knox Press, 1989), 106.

[5] Robert Mulholland, *Shaped by the Word: The Power of Scripture in Spiritual Formation* (Nashville: Upper Room Press, 1985), 109.

[6] Eugene Peterson, *Working the Angles: The Shape of Pastoral Integrity* (Grand Rapids: Eerdmans, 1994), 89.

[7] George Barna, "Re-churching the Unchurched" Seminar (8 March 2001).

[8] Bill Easum, "Evangelism in the 21st Century," *Net Results* Journal (February 2001): 22-25.

[9] Ibid., 23-25

[10] Stanley J. Grenz, "The Quest for a Communal Spirituality in the Postmodern World," *Asbury Theological Journal*, vol. 54, no. 2 (Fall 1999): 41-51.

[11] Adapted from *Explorer*, no. 19 (11 September 2000), an interview with Gary McIntosh, Leadership Network.

[12] Alister Emerson, "Delegation: Key to Leadership," from *Leadership Journal* (Winter 2001): 44-46.

Resources

Church Leadership

Bandy, Tom. *Christianity in Chaos*. Nashville: Abingdon Press, 1999.

_____. *Coaching Change: Breaking Down Resistance and Building Up Hope*. Nashville: Abingdon Press, 2000.

Christensen, Michael. *Equipping the Saints: Mobilizing Laity for Ministry*. Nashville: Abingdon Press, 2000.

Easum, Bill. *Growing Spiritual Redwoods*. Nashville: Abingdon Press, 1998.

_____. *Leadership on the Other Side*. Abingdon Press, 2000

Howe, Leroy. *A Pastor in Every Pew: Equipping laity for Pastoral Care.* Valley Forge: Judson Press, 2000.

McIntosh, Gary, and Samuel D. Rima. *Overcoming the Dark Side of Leadership.* Grand Rapids: Baker Books, 1999.

McLaren, Brian. *A New Kind of Christian.* San Francisco: Jossey-Bass, 2001.

Sweet, Leonard. *Aqua Church.* Grand Rapids:Zondervan Press, 2000.

Spiritual Formation Through Media

Fields, Doug, and Eddie James. *Videos that Teach.* Grand Rapids: Zondervan Publishing House, 1999.

Forbes, Bruce, and Jeffrey Mahan. *Religion and Popular Culture in America.* University of California Press, 2000.

Gire, Ken. *Reflections on the Movies.* Colorado Springs: Victor, 2000.

Jewett, Robert. *Saint Paul at the Movies.* Louisville: Westminster/John Knox Press, 1993.

Johnston, Robert K. *Reel Spirituality: Theology and Film in Dialogue.* Grand Rapids: Baker Books, 2000.

Marsh, C., and G. Ortiz. *Exploring Theology and Film.* Los Angeles: Blackwell, 1997.

McNulty, Edward. *Films and Faith: Forty Discussion Guides.* Topeka, KS: Viaticum Press, 1999.

_____. *Praying the Movies.* Louisville: Geneva Press, 2001.

_____, ed. *Visual Parables, a Monthly Review of Films, Videos, and the Arts.* Topeka, KS: Kash Literary Enterprises.

Miller, Kim, and the Ginghamsburg Church Worship Team. *Handbook for Multi-Sensory Worship.* Nashville: Abingdon Press, 1999.

Stone, Bryan. *Faith and Film: Theological Themes at the Cinema.* Boston: Chalice Press, 2000.

Vaux, Sara Anson. *Finding Meaning at the Movies.* Nashville: Abingdon Press, 1999.

Team-Based Ministry

Bandy, Tom. *Coaching Change: Breaking Down Resistance and Building Up Hope.* Nashville: Abingdon Press, 2000.

Carter, William. *Team Spirituality: A Guide for Staff and Church.* Nashville: Abingdon Press, 1997.

Cladis, George. *Leading Team-Based Churches.* San Francisco: Jossey-Bass Publishers, 1999.

Corderio, Wayne. *Doing Church as a Team.* Honolulu, Hawaii: New Hope Publishers, 1998 and 2000.

Maxwell, John. *The 17 Indispensable Laws of Teamwork.* Nashville: Thomas Nelson, 2001.

Net Results Magazine, "Starting the Shift to Team-Based Organization," February 2001.

Toler, Stan. *The Pastor's Playbook: Coaching Your Team for Ministry.* Boston: Beacon Hill Press, 2000.

Church—A Redemptive Community?
An Open Door for
Secular & Sacred People

"Redeemed, how I love to proclaim it . . . ," one of those old and favorite hymns of many of us raised in a churched culture. We embraced and understood the words and most of the concepts and that seemed sufficient for most. Now that we are living and seeking to minister in what is primarily a postmodern, postChristian, and increasingly secular culture, we need to revisit the truths and concepts of the hymn and translate them so an unchurched culture can understand and embrace. Unfortunately, in many of our current churches we are not manifesting a biblical definition of "redemptive community." It seems to them that we proclaim redemption, but we don't practice it or do so selectively.

Our churches are filled with many lonely people, sitting in parallel pews, looking at the back of each other's heads while yearning to find and experience community. The unchurched and the churched are observing many incidences where our churches are not manifesting redemption or community. For instance:

• Churches, parishes or judicatories are frequently guilty of not treating their staff or pastors very redemptively. Many are being spontaneously fired, often with little known or clarified cause. Such a reaction doesn't frequently include attempts to restore a fallen or ineffective pastor or staff person. They are simply "fired." In more cases than I would like to confess, I hear of churches that all but "kick them out in the street" being told to vacate a parsonage within a few weeks. Or they may be asked to leave after many years of service and ministry, due to staff reorganization and not given much if any notice or severance. Now how redemptive is this? This is the way we treat our pastors and staff. Imagine what we do to members.

- In more than a few cases I've known churches to be anything but redemptive to straying or fallen members; members who might be in a "messy family situation" — divorce, custody battles, family feuds over estate settlement, alcoholism etc. We often alienate ourselves from them or them from us. We push them from leadership without any attempt to restore or assist them in growing through life struggles and turning those struggles into pathways of ministry and healing for others in the church or community. Such tragedies do tend to get communicated and or miscommunicated to the churched and the unchurched people.

Search for a Redemptive Experience

Unchurched persons and many churched persons are looking for connectedness, acceptance, grace and experiences and relationships that are redemptive — that will take something in them that is ugly and worthless and turn it into something of value and significance. Many are on a search for significance. Many need a community of concerned and caring, trusted friends to help them find and stay on the journey of redemption. What experiences and events do you or your congregation currently offers that might help an unbeliever find and follow such a redemptive journey? There are several things we must ask ourselves when trying to answer this question:

- How many unbelievers or unchurched persons do we know or attract by what we are currently doing or how we currently act?
- Why are nonbelievers not attracted to us or our events or programs?
- Are we building bridges are barriers to the unredeemed by who we are and/or what we do?

All of this now becomes part of the Christian education curricula for ministering to and in a secular and postmodern culture. The postmodern world is looking for experiences and relationships that are redemptive and nurturing. Many didn't find it in their families and now they seek to discover and embrace it through other means. In days gone by, we would write a book, print a Sunday School lesson in a quarterly, and it would facilitate Christian education. Now the curricula becomes life experiences and relationships. The books, literature and programs become a place and an opportunity to process life and find God in it.

For instance, Chuck, a friend of a mutual friend, was on a search for truth, for understanding of his struggles in life and faith. He was connected to me as a possible safe place to process some of his struggle. Through countless emails, phone conversations and eventually face to face communication, Chuck began to make some empowering connections that nurtured his self-esteem and self-image that had been distorted due to social and family relationships. His faith was becoming an anchor. During this time he was part of a Bible study group and a mission group. His observation to me was that the dialogue we were having was much more helpful in his faith formation, understanding of Christ's work in his life and family and breaking of unhealthy life patterns than any of those group experiences. I encouraged him to stay in the groups, to continue his prayer and Bible Study as well as our conversations. All were important and a good balance. My point here is that the redemptive dialogue, relationships and experiences seem to be missing from just the printed or programmed curricula. The human experience and the process of theological reflection on life experiences is a vital skill to be learned and practiced in today's world and church. The theological reflection and the relationship became a source of understanding and experience of redemption for Chuck. Through various reflective and non-threatening questions he was able to make some connections between life and faith, pain and relationships that birthed new life in him and brought him relief. I think Chuck and others in this search are teaching us how to build bridges to them instead of barriers — if we'll just listen.

Engagement with Nonbelievers?

George Barna explains from his research, "church leaders will have to better understand why the unchurched don't feel they need organized religion." He further declares, "church leaders will need to find better ways to make the church relevant through programs that help people with their needs, whether that's learning about computers or improving marriages."[1] In an unchurched culture where many confess to be on a spiritual pilgrimage, but who are not interested in the way we do church, how can we become more effective in moving the non-believer or the non-churched person toward a healthy spiritual journey? Seems to me that there are several helpful hints:

- Carve out times and create opportunities to become involved with nonbelievers. Many believers do not really know unbelievers. Many of us have been taught not to associate with them. Pray tell how do we expect to influence them when they don't come to our church meetings (where most of us spend most of our time and energy) and we don't know them? In an unchurched culture we have to see building relationships with nonbelievers as a primary challenge and priority. Serving on church committees might have to give way to engaging with nonbelievers as an avenue of Christian service.
- Create opportunities to meet and build trusting, healthy relationships with nonbelievers. Consider . . .
    - Who are the nonbelievers you encounter on a regular basis in your daily life?
    - What common points of interest might you share with those persons (leisure activities, family status, vocation, children, weight loss or health challenges, investments, gardening, etc.)?
- Pray and create a prayer team to bathe these relationships and opportunities in prayer. Keep them aware of prayer needs and ministry needs.
- Build in accountability with your support base to insure that the relationship stays healthy. Remember when helping someone else ends up hurting you it becomes an unhealthy relationship.
- Try to understand their language, their search, the spiritual challenges and life needs. So often we only pay attention when they use our "church language." I'm learning that many times their spiritual search is very authentic; even though they may use language we are not familiar with or comfortable with to describe their journey. For instance, working with Randy, a 30-year-old spiritually minded person, but unchurched, used "getting into the flow of life, or following the energy of the universe." Such caused me at first to think he was a "new-ager." I came to discover, after listening and asking for

clarification, that he was meaning the same thing I meant when I spoke of the Holy Spirit's work in my life. He just didn't have the language or comfort with "my religious language." You see I learned that he had been part of church in his youth and had a bad experience and didn't want to revisit those memories triggered by "my religious words."

• Storytelling becomes a significant pathway to understanding, ministry and redemptive experiences. Learning to facilitate story telling, the sharing of life experiences, captures the post-modern world and creates a forum for connecting their/our stories to "His-story." When a natural connection surfaces between a life experience and a biblical truth or story, it becomes a great teachable moment on many fronts. After making the connection frequently enough, it seems to create an interest to do their own biblical research. Again, let me suggest that this type of experience is a key missing piece in Christian education curricula framework for the secular culture and postmodern world.

We are living in a day when we must not think *church*, rather we must think *missions* if the church is to survive in this postmodern age. The challenge is to present God's good news to all of humankind. To do this in a pluralistic culture we face the challenge of contextualization. How do we preserve the integrity of the Good News and communicate in ways those different groups from various backgrounds can understand enough to embrace. After all it must be communicable for it to be news.

Many argue that we must not contextualize. Let me be clear. I'm not suggesting we change the message, but rather insure that the message is clearly understood by our openness to changing methods and even language.

There is a precedence in scripture for contextualization. The very issue of God coming to us in human flesh — the incarnation — is the best example of contextualizing I know. We can also find contextualization in Paul's ministry. Consider Acts 14:8-20 when they encourage problems with language and culture when taking the message to Lystra. Not only did they encounter cultural dissonance but faced having to change their language to be more effective in their ministry in Lystra. Should we do no less?

Experiencing Authenticity of Faith and Life

Generation X and the millennial generations are attracted by, and want to be part of, genuineness and authenticity of faith and life. Much of what the builders and boomers have created in our church unfortunately doesn't see authenticity as a vital part of our church experience. We have built buildings and programs and invested ourselves in missions. The church that will survive the builders and boomers generation is being called to invest in each other's lives, to walk together on an authentic search for spiritual maturity and the abundant life. Creating centralized learning experiences at an agreed upon time and place and topic met the needs of the builders and to some degree the boomer and buster generations. However, now Christian education is being pushed, by the new generations, to a much less institutionally focused approach, more decentralized, more relational, less driven by printed predetermined literature. What will engage the new generations seems to be around life issues that emerge throughout the week and touch their daily life experiences — work, play, family issues, investing issues, relationships, addictions, dysfunction, etc. The curriculum is a group of persons willing to share this journey and struggle for authenticity and stabilizing solutions to their life challenges. The growing degree of diversity in which this generation lives pushes the limits of a centralized narrowly focused curriculum agenda. It is increasingly clear that the search for truth and spiritual formation manifests itself differently in different generations and cultures. While scripture is truth and Christ is the visible incarnation of that truth, a shifting of our culture takes us back to the birthing of the New Testament Church in the book of Acts. This redemptive community had several viable characteristics we must return to if we want to speak to a post–Christian, postmodern culture.

An effective Christian education ministry for our postmodern, postChristian world has several basic ingredients. These ingredients are modeled in the early church as described in the book of Acts. Let me restate principles of effective Christian education in a secular culture. Christian education is:

- Relational
- Flexible and spontaneous
- Focused on life issues
- Based in authenticity
- An intentional search for truth and wholeness
- Decentralized more often than not
- Propelled by theological reflection & story
- Nurtured by reflection on story & multimedia challenges
- Rooted in truth
- Life-transforming

If we can recapture these vital ingredients for Christian education in this secular age, we will have a better chance of speaking to the generations that will carry the Good News into the twenty-first century. The generations that will carry our Christian faith into the new century are not nearly as interested in an age graded Sunday School as they are an authentic search for faith and truth among persons who want to be on that journey. They are not nearly as interested in being at a "church building" for their faith formation experiences as they desire to "experience church and build authentic trustworthy relationships." They are not nearly as interested in preserving the rituals of the past as they are owning and embracing rituals and traditions that have meaning to their digital and fast paced life experiences.

Am I suggesting that the church doesn't need to get together in an assembly for worship and equipping? Certainly not. I'm suggesting that this corporate or institutionally-based model, where we meet together several times a week, may be fading away for now. What might be emerging is similar to the decentralized house churches, small group focused, highly relational models we see in the book of Acts. This will be supplemented by periodic corporate gatherings, probably in a large meeting place like a school auditorium. This might be complemented by small focused worship experiences in a variety of worship styles that are intentional about speaking the message in ways that various people groups, with various learning or worship styles can grow.

The issue becomes not how we can preserve the church we have known and loved and has nurtured us to where we are today. The issue is that found in the book of Acts. How can we engage a growing secular culture in ways that will invite them and encourage them to explore the Christian faith? How can we incarnate the Good News of the Gospel so that the secular post-modern world might have a better chance to experience what we know about redemption, about grace, about mercy and a community of faith? We're not after compromising the Gospel, we are about discovering methods that will help connect people to faith in ways that allows and encourages them to grow from where they are to where God would have them be — "mature in the faith." Yes, "while we were yet sinners Christ died for us." He met us where we were/are in order that we might come to know Him in all His fullness. We can do no less in this world full of lost souls. "Redeemed by the Blood of the Lamb, Redeemed in His infinite mercies — His child and forever I am."

Note

[1]Julie Kay, "Barna: Churches Must Change," *The Advocate Online* (12 April 2001).

APPENDIX A
Distinctives in Each Disciple-Making Phase

	Come See	Follow Me	Be With Me	Remain in Me
Scripture	John 1:38-39	Mark 1:16-17	Mark 3:13-14	John 15:4
Time	3 Months	9 Months	22 Months	Lifetime
Intent	• To attract and win to himself • To build beliefs and some priorities	• To train for task • To build habits and basic character	• To deploy as disciple-makers • To deepen basic habits and develop new ones	• To replace Himself • To continue the development of Christ-likeness without forgetting the basics
Disciples' Involvement	• Mostly watching • Somewhat involved • Did not lead	• Somewhat watched • Quite involved • Did not lead	• Quite involved • Did a lot of leading	• Involved in leading leaders
Commitment	• Casual occasional attendance	• Constantly present	• Willing to die/give all to follow as long as Jesus was present	• Intrinsically motivated to the death
Content		Mostly the Same	Truth But Deepening	With Time
Summary	• Tell Them What • Tell Them Why	• Show Them How • Do it With Them	• Let Them Do It • Deploy Them	• Multiplication • Continual Growth

From T-NET International Leadership Training. Used by Permission from Bob Gilliam, President.
For more information call 1-800-995-5362 or visit www.tnetwork.com and read Jesus Christ the Disciplemaker,
The Disciple Making Church by Bill Hull, Revell Press.

Findley Edge and I worked several years ago through the scriptures in the New Testament that speak to the salvation experience. Let me share the chart we ended up with for your review as a biblical backdrop for this chapter.

APPENDIX B
Passages Related to Salvation in the Gospels

Passages that seem to indicate that salvation is simple and easy:

Matt. 11:28-30 My yoke is easy and my burden is light.

Matt. 18:1-4 Except ye become converted and become as little children, ye shall not enter into the Kingdom of Heaven.

Matt. 19:13-14 (Mark 10:13-16) Suffer the little children, and forbid them not to come unto me; for of such is the kingdom of heaven.

Mark 9:36-37 And he took a child, and set him in the midst of them, and when he had taken him in his arms, he said unto them, Whosoever shall receive one of such children in my name, receiveth me, and whosoever shall receive me, receiveth not me, but him that sent me.

Luke 18:16-17 Suffer the little children to come. . . Whosoever shall not receive the kingdom of God as a little child shall in no wise enter therein.

Luke 23:43 Verily I say unto thee, Today shalt thou be with me in paradise.

John 1:12 As many as received him, to them gave he power to become the sons of God, even to them that believe on his name.

John 3:16 For God so loved the world that he gave his only begotten Son, that whosoever believeth in him should not perish, but have everlasting life.

John 3:18 He that believeth not is condemned already, because he hath not believed in the name of the only begotten Son of God.

John 12:44 He that believeth on me believeth not on me, but on him that sent me.

Passages that seem to indicate that salvation is difficult and complex:

Matt. 3:7-12 (Luke 3: 7-9) (John the Baptist) Bring forth fruits meet for repentance... Every tree which bringeth not forth good fruit is hewn down and cast into the fire.

Matt. 6:14-15 If ye forgive men their trespasses, your heavenly Father will also forgive you; But if ye forgive not men their trespasses, neither will you Father forgive your trespasses.

Matt. 7:13-14 Enter ye in at the strait gate, for wide is the gate, and broad is the way that leadeth to destruction, and many there be which go in thereat; Because strait is the gate and narrow is the way which leadeth unto life, and few there be that find it.

Matt. 7:16, 20 Ye shall know them by their fruits.

Matt. 7:21-23 Not every one that saith unto me, Lord, Lord, shall enter into the kingdom of heaven but he that doeth the will of my Father which is in heaven.; Many will say to me in that day, Lord, Lord, have we not prohesied in thy name? and in thy name done many wonderful works? And then will I profess unto them, I never knew you; depart from me, ye that work iniquity.

Matt. 7:24-27 (Luke 6:46-49) Therefore whosoever feareth these sayings of mine and doeth them, I will liken him unto a wise man which built his house upon a rock.

Matt. 8:22 Jesus said to him, Follow me and let the dead bury their dead.

Matt. 10:22 He that endureth to the end shall be saved.

Matt. 10:32-38 Whosoever therefore shall confess me before men, will I confess also before my Father which is in heaven. But whosoever shall deny me before men, him will I also deny before my Father which is in heaven... I came not to send peace, but a sword... He that loveth father or mother more than me is not worthy of me, and he that loveth son or daughter more than me is not worthy of me. And he that taketh not his cross and followeth after me is not worthy of me. He that findeth his life shall lose it, and he that loseth his life for my sake shall find it.

Matt. 12:30 He that is not with me is against me; and he that gathereth not with me scattereth abroad.

Matt. 12:33 Either make the tree good; or else make the tree corrupt; for the tree is known by its fruit.

Matt. 13:1-9 A sower went forth to sow... Some fell by the way side, and the fowls came and devoured them up... because they had no root, they withered away... Some fell among thorns and the thorns sprung up, and choked them... But others fell on good ground, and brought forth fruit... Who hath ears to hear let him hear.

Matt. 16:24 Then said Jesus unto his disciples, If any man will come after me, let him deny himself, and take up his cross, and follow me.

Matt. 19:16-22 (Mark 10:17-22. Luke 18:18-22) What shall I do that I may have eternal life? . . . Jesus said unto him, . . . sell that thou hast . . . and follow me.

Matt. 19:19-24 (Luke 18: 23-25) It is easier for a camel to go through the eye of a needle than for a rich man to enter into the kingdom of God.

Matt. 21:28-32 Go work today in my vineyard... Whither of them did the will of the Father?

Matt. 21:33-43 Therefore I say unto you, the kingdom shall be taken from you, and given to a nation bringing forth the fruits thereof.

Matt. 25:37-46 (Parable of the Judgment) Inasmuch as ye have done it unto one of the least of these my brethren, ye have done it unto me. . . Inasmuch as ye did it not to one of the least of these, ye did it not to me.

Luke 13:23-24 Then said one unto him, Lord, are there few that be saved? And he said unto them, Strive to enter in at the strait gate, for many, I say unto you, will seek to enter in, and shall not be able.

Luke 14:25-27 And there went great multitudes with him, and he turned, and said to them, If any man come to me, and hate not his father, and mother, and wife, and children, and brethren, and sister, yea, and his own life also, he cannot be my disciple. And whosoever doth not bear his cross, and come after me, cannot be my disciple.

Luke 14:28-33 For which of you, intending to build a tower, sitteth not down first, and counteth the cost, whether he have sufficient to finish it . . . So likewise, whosoever he be of you that forsaketh not all that he hath, he cannot be my disciple.

John 12:20-26 Except a grain of wheat fall into the ground and die, it abideth alone; but if it die, it bringeth forth much fruit. He that loveth his life shall lose it; and he that hateth his life in this world shall keep it unto life eternal. If any man serve me, let him follow me.

John 14:15 If ye love me, keep my commandments.

John 14:23-24 If any man love me, he will keep my words; and my Father will love him, and we will come unto him, and make our abode with him. He that loveth me not keepeth not my sayings.

John 15:2 Every branch in me that beareth not fruit he taketh away; and every branch that beareth fruit, he purgeth it, that it may bring forth more fruit.

Passages that are difficult to classify in these categories:

Matt. 4:17 From that time Jesus began to preach, and to say, Repent; for the kingdom of heaven is at hand.

Matt. 20: 1-16 And when they came that were hired about the eleventh hour, they received every man a penny.

Mark 10:45 For the Son of Man came not to be ministered unto, but to minister, and to give his life a ransom for man.

Mark 12:34 Thou art not far from the kingdom of God.

Luke 13:3 Except ye repent, ye shall all likewise perish.

Luke 19:10 For the Son of man is come to seek and to save that which is lost.

APPENDIX C
Moving from Program Base Design to Function Base Design

Key Question: Who are the people groups our church is called to attract or minister to? How can we meet them where they are and provide experiences or relationships to move them to becoming a healthy disciple of Christ?

FUNCTIONS TO ACCOMPLISH WITH EACH GROUP

GROUPS TO:	ATTRACTION (Come and See Phase)	ASSIMILATION (Come and Follow Me)	DISCIPLING (Come and Be With Me)	DEPLOYING (Come and Abide in Me)
ATTRACT				
Unbelieving Spouses of Believers	Identify them via observation, survey, internet, fishing or hunting competitions	Sporting Teams, business groups, Bible Studies, building cyber-communities	Mentoring Relationships, Bible Study, Group Studies, Group membership explore	Become mentor for others; Create appropriate entry points
Inactive Church Members	Search for life pinches; Build non-threatening relationships via leisure activities; Listen don't judge	Invite to 4 X 4 luncheons, activities. Explore spiritual based questions	Invite to 'grief' seminars, churchwide fellowships; Invite to be part of dinner theater; Invite to group they are interested in	Retool for ministry to other in actives
Parents with Aging Parents	Team for 'caring for caregivers'; Community agencies for Senior Adults	Seminar or group for caregivers; Offer team for respite care	Invite to appropriate Bible studies or support groups	Begin support group or counseling or respite care ministries
Young Couples	Marriage Fair	Bootcamp for Dads	Men's/Women's Group	Community Based Marriage Fair; Parenting Seminar

Key Question: Who is already attracted to (in) our church or church activities but doesn't feel like they belong? How can we be intentional about meeting them where they are and create experiences to help them become a healthy disciple of Christ?

FUNCTIONS TO ACCOMPLISH IN THE BODY OF CHRIST

GROUPS TO:	ATTRACTION (Come and See Phase)	ASSIMILATION (Come and Follow Me)	DISCIPLING (Come and Be With Me)	DEPLOYING (Come and Abide in Me)
ASSIMILATE				
Parents of DayCare/Kindergarten Children	Letter of invitation, Pastor/staff open house, invite to join teams.	Network with other parents in similar circumstances.	Provide biblical information about parenting and process opportunities.	Enlist and train to mentor other parents/ marriages. Invite to participate in mission opportunity.
Faculty of Local School	Be intentional about presence of church at school activities.	Discover connections already in school and intentionally build networks and relationships.	Provide opportunities for exploring biblical truths that relate to educational challenges.	Commissioning service and covenant with school faculty. Create Prayer chains for and with faculty.
Home Schooling Families/children/ parents	Identify, network and create support opportunities and resources.	Plan workshops, networking and social times for parents & students.	Affirm Christian education in the home, parental commitment through biblical study.	Commission them, build covenant with them. Create mission opportunities for them. Establish Prayer Chair.
Newcomers to Church Membership	Build community among newcomers Introduce to facilities and programming.	Build relationships between establish church and new church. Invite into leadership roles and mentoring relationships.	Offer opportunities to clarify their commitments and network with others making similar commitments.	Assure prayer, support for their journey and ministry. Help them discover call, giftedness and ministry.

Key Question: Who is already attracted to, and assimilated into life of the congregation, but needs to take next steps in becoming an informed disciple? What experiences can be provided to help them move forward in their journey?

FUNCTIONS TO ACCOMPLISH IN THE BODY OF CHRIST

GROUPS TO:	ATTRACTION (Come and See Phase)	ASSIMILATION (Come and Follow Me)	DISCIPLING (Come and Be With Me)	DEPLOYING (Come and Abide in Me)
DISCIPLE				
Sunday School Leaders	Invite them to take care of their spiritual needs while teaching others.	Create opportunities and expectations for their ongoing community building and training.	Covenant with them to encourage and guide their spiritual formation and modeling of healthy discipleship.	Provide opportunities for involvement in mission and theological reflection on their teaching roles.
Choir Members	Covenant with them and invite them into spiritual formation.	Build accountable teams and community among choirs, ensembles etc.	Provide training and opportunities to reflect on scripture, hymn texts and life experiences together.	Provide consistent mission opportunities for sharing musical skills. Create entry points for unchurched among all choirs/groups.
Committee Members	Build teams around calling, mission and giftedness.	Build accountable communities and pastoral care among all team members.	Share experiences of committee ministries and guide theological reflection and affirmation of that ministry. Help them see their function in the body.	How can their 'inward focused' ministry be translated into mission endeavors? How can they mentor/apprentice the next leaders?

Key Question: What group in our church has found their place in the congregation, feels comfortable and like they belong, but are yet to capture the next step of the Christian journey into mission/ministry involvement? What experiences can we provide that will move them forward in mission involvement and maturity as healthy disciple of Christ?

FUNCTIONS TO ACCOMPLISH IN THE BODY OF CHRIST

GROUPS TO: DEPLOY	ATTRACTION (Come and See Phase)	ASSIMILATION (Come and Follow Me)	DISCIPLING (Come and Be With Me)	DEPLOYING (Come and Abide in Me)
Deacons	Congregational education about function of deacon.	Invite persons seen as servant leaders to dialogue about deacon ministry or apprentice with them.	Create atmosphere for mentoring and accountability relationships among deacons.	Fashion deacons into ministry teams accountable for co-pastoring the congregation.
Families	Use language and programming that targets todayís family structures and schedules.	Provide atmosphere and opportunity for mentoring relationships among families and family members.	Create mentoring relationships for marriages and forums for families dealing with similar life issues/passages.	Create forums for families to go on mission together and reach out to other families in their sphere of influence.
Christian Businesspersons	Create forums for support and resourcing around subjects of interest to business leaders.	Create appropriate opportunities for business persons to explore the faith in the context of business. Be sure to model excellence.	Create affinity groups for business persons to explore the implications of Christianity on business services.	Engage persons in missions utilizing their areas of expertise and calling.

APPENDIX D
Moving from Program Base Design to Function Base Design

GROUPS TO:	ATTRACTION	ASSIMILATION	DISCIPLING	DEPLOYING
ATTRACT				
ASSIMILATE				

FUNCTIONS TO ACCOMPLISH WITH EACH GROUP

FUNCTIONS TO ACCOMPLISH WITH EACH GROUP

GROUPS TO:	ATTRACTION	ASSIMILATION	DISCIPLING	DEPLOYING
DISCIPLE				
DEPLOY